STRATEGIES
for
SURVIVAL

Using business know-how
to make our social system work

STRATEGIES
for
SURVIVAL

DAVID F. LINOWES

amacom

A DIVISION OF AMERICAN MANAGEMENT ASSOCIATIONS

TO DOROTHY

International standard book number: 0-8144-5326-0
Library of Congress catalog card number: 73-75673
First printing

PREFACE

"It must be terrible to live in the United States today. I understand people are afraid to walk in the streets at night in the downtown areas in many of your cities." The speaker was a middle-class Greek citizen of Athens, who spoke with visible concern in a sympathetic voice. He was addressing me in the fall of 1971 while I was on a mission to Greece under the auspices of the U.S. Department of State.

Hearing this caused me to pause and ponder; the experience was unique. In all my travels to countries throughout the world, both officially and unofficially during the past quarter century, never before was I given sympathy because I was an American. Always, in the past, I was the envy of the people I met, whether they spoke French, German, Japanese, or Hindustani. What had happened to us in the United States? Indeed, what is still happening?

For decades it has been apparent to many thoughtful Americans that our social institutions are not responding to the needs of our people—too many schools are not educating, too many prisons are not reforming, too many poverty programs are not relieving need. The cities, states, and federal government keep spending more and more hundreds of billions of dollars, yet conditions do not improve.

There must be a solution somewhere, if we could but find it. Seven years ago I began to grope for an answer. I undertook to examine the other group of mammoth institutions that exist in our society—industrial organizations—to search for a clue that might lead to the means for correcting the decay that afflicts so many of our government and social agencies. Industry is prosperous; it thrives in productivity and profitability. Industry is also massive, but industrial organizations flourish. This book is my humble effort to apply the successful practices of industry to our failing nonprofit organizations. The need is critical.

Many have had important influences on my thinking, which resulted in the development of the subject matter contained in this book. To all of them, I express my deep gratitude.

I would be remiss, however, if I did not specifically acknowledge John W. Gardner for the thoughts he triggered during our discussions, first when he was president of the Carnegie Foundation, and then during his tenure as secretary of the Department of Health, Education, and Welfare.

My appreciation goes to Senator Walter F. Mondale, Clayton Fritchey, and David W. Ewing for the encouragement they gave me to publish my concepts of Socio-Economic Management. My thanks to Norman Cousins for his gracious guidance after the work was completed and before the publisher was selected.

Raymond Dreyfack's assistance was invaluable in the research and preparation of the manuscript. Mrs. Judi Rieger performed her secretarial responsibilities in retyping the several drafts of each chapter with her usual contagious enthusiasm. My sincere appreciation to each of them.

DAVID F. LINOWES

CONTENTS

1

THE TUG OF PEACE

America—as these words are being written—is embroiled in a giant tug of peace. A heated battle is raging between this nation's bureaucrats and its social reformers.

In one fortress we see the entrenched mediocrities who are convinced they're on the right track and have a good thing going: maximum ease and minimum accountability. Composed mainly of shortsighted politicians and ineffective administrators, this group espouses no cause more fervently than that of maintaining the status quo. Their arsenal of weapons is impressive: custom and tradition, the established hierarchy, public apathy, resistance to change—familiar deterrents to progress that have served them well in the past.

Manning the opposing battlement are an abundance of dedicated men and women who recognize the burning fact that without quick and effective social improvement our future democratic way of life may be no fact at all. Their arsenal, if they would only reach out and grasp its weapons, is vastly more formidable than the bureaucratic arsenal. These are the strategies for survival, which I will discuss in detail throughout this book. They are simple and obvious. And they are not only possible, they have been widely tested and amply proven. Most important of all, they are ours for the taking.

The basic strategies are neither revolutionary nor startlingly new. It is where and how they are to be applied that is new. They are familiar to efficient executives in business and to students of business management. They will be recognized by any person who has held an executive post in a well-run corporation. The strategies are embodied in such operational words as organization and planning, goals and standards, audit, measurement, motivation, innovation, and accountability.

1

The principles have been conscientiously applied by successful and progressive organizations for decades. This takes in thousands of modern corporations and perhaps a handful of government and nonprofit institutions across the nation. In my view, this is one of our most pressing problems today—that the strategies for survival (and healthy growth) used so extensively in business are completely ignored or at best applied on a disorganized and limited basis in the nonprofit sector.

Sick societies do not break down overnight. Instead, an insidious process of erosion takes place. A favorite word of those who are attempting to pound home to us the alternative to social reform is survival. Is it too strong a word? Melodramatic overstatement? I think not. We are surrounded on all sides with mountains of evidence to prove that if we continue for much longer on our current disaster course, a total collapse of this democratic nation could well take place. And ironically, deep down, a majority of Americans seem to share this opinion.

In early 1971, a survey was conducted by the Gallup organization for Potomac Associates, Inc., a nonprofit research group. An extensive cross section of the American public was polled, and 47 percent of the respondents said they felt that our present unrest is likely to lead to "a real breakdown in this country." That's almost one out of every two Americans, and a majority of those with an opinion. (Fifteen percent gave "don't know" answers.)

One of the key reasons cited for the breakdown: "Our traditional way of doing things is not working and some basic changes are needed."

From a meeting of mayors in New York in 1971 came the conclusion that: "First, the crisis of the cities was the major threat to the security of the nation . . . second, that the bankruptcy and anarchy of the cities was underestimated by the people and by the state and federal governments; and third . . . that their campaign for President Nixon's revenue sharing and tax reform programs was failing." The picture these mayors reported on was called "devastating" by James Reston, a highly respected columnist and vice-president of *The New York Times*.

New York Mayor John V. Lindsay capsulized the general

mayoral reaction when he said: "Not since the Depression have the goals of State and locality been so readily summed up in one word: survival." So we are back where we started again.

If anyone thinks the word survival is too strong, have him go visit a ghetto. There, have him talk with a telephone repairman who won't make a call unless someone is standing by. Have him talk with a teacher who refuses to teach without police protection. Have him talk with a postman who will deliver the mail only if accompanied: One man drops letters in boxes, the other stands guard over both the mail and his companion. Have him talk with a fireman who won't put out a fire unless he is covered by the police and, sometimes, the National Guard.

Nor is mindless violence our only problem. In the midst of unprecedented affluence we find our cities hovering on the edge of bankruptcy. Our welfare system, described by President Nixon as a "monstrous consuming outrage," is but one example. In New York City alone, one out of every eight persons is on the relief rolls, with the number of cases mounting. As Boston's Mayor Kevin White once put it: "Governing U.S. cities is a losing ball game."

We are all of us the losers. Not only cities, but states and counties too are being squeezed beyond their financial ability to respond to human needs. And all the while our national debt keeps rising dangerously, with adequate solutions to urgent problems no closer than before.

In government today, the approach is to look upward for relief. City officials now turn to the state for help with such burdens as welfare, education, and crime control. And state officials turn in desperation to the federal government.

But even if the cries of our nation's mayors and governors were heeded in Washington, that would offer no real or lasting solution. America's underprivileged millions want food and jobs and hope. Its middle millions want protection of body and assets. To them it makes no difference at all if the country's programs and projects are mismanaged by city, state, or federal institutions. In the final reckoning, the solution to the crisis of the seventies lies, not in who tries to do the job, but in how it is done.

THE STATE OF THE ART OF SURVIVAL

What is being done in the seventies to help insure our freedom, economic solvency, and physical security in the eighties?

Many thoughtful and earnest reformers in government, business, and the academic community are sounding the call for survival. But it is being muted by the roar of the status quo advocates, who play life by the numbers instead of by human needs. They cling to tradition with tenacity. In setting up programs and projects, they think in terms of quantity of beds to be filled, diplomas to be ground out, cell blocks to fill, mouths to feed, housing units to occupy—rather than in terms of how well the programs are working to reduce the number of unfulfilled needs. They know what was done in the past and whether it has worked or not. They provide more of the same for the future, as often as not superimposing disorganization on chaos in the process. Their guideline is numbers and their god is the budget.

But money alone, however vital its role in the scheme of restructuring, cannot convert mismanagement to good management unless the system is reformed to include the proven basics of effective management. As Dr. Lawrence S. Ritter, professor of Finance at New York University's Graduate School of Business Administration, puts it:

It has become a staple of social commentary in recent years to urge a "reordering of national priorities." Typically, this takes the form of recommending that state and local government spending, federal nondefense spending, and homebuilding be expanded to alleviate pressing social problems.

However, the quantitative dimensions of such increases are rarely specified. Similarly unidentified are the areas where spending, public or private, might have to be curtailed to permit an expansion in the recommended directions. One cannot help suspecting that a large part of the reason for almost complete unanimity on the subject of reordered priorities is that the phrase itself has become little more than a platitude. Devoid of solid content, it floats serenely above debate.

From universities, prisons, hospitals, and federal, state and city agencies, the voice of the requisitioner is heard throughout the land. Along with the pleas come dire predictions. Without more money to operate, critical services will be curtailed, needs will go unmet. The overriding goal of our nonprofit institutions is continued appropriations. And when the appropriations are continued, the needs are still unmet.

We have been riding this pay-out route for years. It is no panacea. Certainly experience has taught us by now that money cannot buy solutions. It cannot produce results where the foundation for results has not been established.

Job training is a prime example. Despite the millions of dollars poured into a myriad of ad hoc programs in the sixties, the number of qualified unemployed has not on the whole significantly increased. The nation's welfare rolls are more swollen than ever.

As with job training, education in general has received appropriations to spare during the past decade. In the sixties our schools asked for and got, says Alvin C. Eurich, president of the Academy for Educational Development, Inc., tremendous increases in local, state, and federal support of education at all levels. During the sixties the schools' income rose faster than the GNP. In spite of all the money, our schools and colleges have not kept up with our changing society. Indeed, during this decade of affluence, they slipped from first to second place as a major educational enterprise. Eurich notes that television is now number one. By the time the average American completes high school today, he has spent only 11,000 hours in school, and 15,000—4,000 hours more—in front of the television set!

Inevitably, we return to the basics of management. If these are missing, the system will falter. Our system developed on basic assumptions which are no longer valid. The first false assumption is that more money for education is bound to make it more effective. By force-feeding our institutions without making any basic changes, we merely magnified antiquated practices without improving the operation. It is a pattern we see duplicated throughout the nonprofit sector of our society, a pattern which, if applied to business, would quickly lead a corporation to ruin.

TAKING OFF THE BLINDERS

Charles L. Schultze, former Bureau of the Budget director, and a team of Brookings Institution economists warn of a dearth of resources ahead for tackling critical national needs, such as the polluted environment, the decaying central cities, the financial problems of the schools and colleges, the remaining poverty and the massive welfare problem.

Impressive economic growth is predicted for the United States in the years ahead, but the tax revenues generated by this growth are already required by existing problems. The Brookings study suggests that acute social needs cannot be met without either raising taxes or cutting lower-priority government programs. But there are strongly entrenched interests ready to defend every part of the budget—and to fight for more.

Nor will the defense be predicated on measured performance or proven potential to fulfill unmet needs. It will be based, if the status quo persists, on the worn and ancient numbers game. So, even if continued funding *were* the solution to our nation's social ills—which mounting evidence vehemently denies—it is quite apparent that an impasse must be reached in the not too distant future. Something, or someone, has to give. If history is any criterion, it won't be the in-group of bureaucrats.

A thought-provoking question is asked by Leonard S. Silk of *The New York Times:* "Is the conventional economics of the nineteen-thirties through the nineteen-sixties adequate to the sense of the seventies as to what economic well-being really means?" His own reply:

The National Environmental Policy Act of 1969 recognizes the "profound impact" on society of population growth, high-density urbanization, industrial expansion, resource exploitation and technological advances. And it calls upon the Government, in cooperation with other public and private organizations, to use all practicable means "to create and maintain conditions under which man and nature can exist in productive harmony, and fulfill the social, economic and other requirements of present and future generations of Americans."

But the economic models and the nation's economic policies have barely begun to take account of the new sense of "the requisites of well-being." The simple and obvious basics of Socio-

Economic Management as they are outlined in this book would *force* such adherence by virtue of the system's controls. Goals and standards would be directed to proven requisites as they are in industry, and performance would be monitored, evaluated, and reported accordingly. And funding would be based on results.

What other choice do we have if "free enterprise" is to persist as something more than a platitude? It has become fairly obvious that the hit-or-missocracy of decades past will never do for the decades to come. The seething millions who are locked into America's ghettos and barrios have made it clear they will no longer accept it passively. Millions of students, the children of the affluent, the young people we are presumably grooming to take over our society, have made it equally clear. And there is rising evidence that the ranks of dissenters are being increasingly swelled by millions of taxpaying consumers, businessmen, educators, and thoughtful citizens from all walks of life who, with one eye on the spending and the other on results, have become disenchanted with the tired cliches of tenacious nonactivists. If something constructive doesn't happen soon, it will result in much more drastic interference with private enterprise than we have ever seen.

One problem today—and a leading cause of campus and ghetto extremist attitudes—is our concentration on corporate profitability with at best little thought given to social profitability. This may have sufficed for the forties and fifties. But if it continues much longer into the seventies, corporate gains will be thinned down to the point where a major portion of the pie will be earmarked as the price for social mismanagement.

What we desperately need are ways and means of improving social earnings (fulfilled human needs) along with traditional corporate earnings. Part of the solution lies with technology, the very phenomenon that has contributed to so many of the problems.

Considerable rancor is felt by students, conservationists, and other critics, who dwell on the adverse effects of technology—air-polluting automobiles, smokestacks, oil spills, and the like. Nowhere else in the world, it seems, are science and technology held in such low regard.

What is too often overlooked is technology's vast potential for not only de-polluting our environment, but for upgrading the level of social management. I refer specifically to those aspects of technology that deal with management systems and management information—computer technology, the technology of cost effectiveness, and accounting technology.

As famed anthropologist Margaret Mead made clear in a television interview with WNBC's Edwin Newman, technology works two ways. What we must do, she explained, is set technologists "to devising ways in which change will no longer be so dangerous as it is at present. That means designing types of reactors that will not pollute. It means designing automobiles that will not pollute, and it means designing highways in such a way that they don't wreck communities and things of this sort. I think we can only cure technology with more technology, but a technology applied in the interests of man instead of technology for technology's sake as we have had in the recent past."

Part of the new technology Dr. Mead refers to would, in my opinion, include the proven tools of business and their application to our social institutions, which presumably have been created to serve mankind.

WHAT ARE WE DOING WRONG?

We are living today in a crisis-oriented society. The only time we grow apprehensive about performance is during an emergency. And by that time the apprehension often borders on panic.

When there is a riot on campus, we respond, as often as not, with an ad hoc commission. We do the same thing when desperate prison inmates rebel, when parents and schoolchildren strike, when welfare recipients squat defiantly on the floors of our social institutions.

This does not imply that we respond properly, thoughtfully, or adequately. We respond in a hurry because circumstances compel us to do so. But with conflicting forces and pressures at work, bitterness and animosity rampant, and special interests with one-track objectives applying pressure, rush decisions are apt to be rash decisions.

We cannot correct overnight, and on a makeshift basis, the social ills that have taken years to develop. We go through the old familiar hassles again and again, and after the excitement of riot or strike is over, we return to the status quo.

The main problem lies in the system itself. The great bulk of our national, state, and local programs—the promises and rhetoric notwithstanding—are undertaken without full knowledge of what they should accomplish and for whom. The tools of monitoring and evaluation are not put to use. The criterion is numbers, the great idol, "How many?"

But the truth of the matter has been repeatedly borne out by experience. In social programs, we cannot fully nor adequately measure the costs and the benefits when our sole criterion is dollars or units of output. There is a need for more understanding of what an agency's purposes and goals are—understanding followed by definition, accountability, and public reporting for all to see. Clearly, in our nation's health, educational, housing, job training, crime control and poverty programs, dollar profits are not the goal. It is thus inappropriate to relate dollar input to the traditionally used quantification of output standards.

The goals of restructuring are clear even if some of the goals of our programs and projects are hazy. We must re-dimension our institutions. We must have a practical and controlled system for managing our social problems and assessing our solutions. Otherwise, enormous sums will continue to be spent, and however large, and to whatever degree they strip the economy, they still will not be adequate to the task. In the final analysis, we must relate our dollars to our achievements.

TAKING UP THE TOOLS

After spending five frustrating years at the pulsing hub of social mismanagement, John W. Gardner, former secretary of Health, Education and Welfare, became convinced that only an aroused and organized citizenry can revitalize "The System" and change the nation's disastrous course. This was not a sudden revelation. I recall clearly in discussions with Dr. Gardner as far back as 1965 that he was then viewing with great concern the complex, involved groupings of our society and how these were stifling human initiative and true progress.

In mid-1970, following through on his conviction, Gardner launched Common Cause, "a citizens' lobby designed to bring pressure through the political process to reform and redesign government so that it will be more responsive to today's needs. . . ." Membership rocketed as the concept captured the imaginations of hundreds of thousands of concerned Americans. Newspapers across the country carried the story of Gardner's efforts to bring about a political renaissance in our time. Numbered among Common Cause's crusades: a vigorous stand against the outdated and paralyzing seniority system in Congress, a suit against both major political parties for violating federal campaign spending statutes, new approaches to the problems of war, poverty, civil rights, and other pressing issues.

The rallying cry of Common Cause as stated in the group's own literature is: "Not a third party but a third force." A new force is also needed to make the management of our nonprofit enterprises coordinated and viable.

Common Cause is dedicated to the cleansing and modernization of America's political system. Socio-Economic Management is dedicated to the cleansing and modernization of the agencies and institutions that operate to make the system work.

Common Cause appeals primarily to the man in the street and counts heavily on the power of the ballot. Socio-Economic Management addresses itself to America's leaders, elected and appointed, most of whom are dedicated men and women of integrity who would otherwise pursue occupations that are more rewarding financially. It appeals to those individuals at the helm of our nation's social agencies, the program directors, planners, administrators, government officials, and budget designers. And it appeals to the managers and businessmen who possess the knowledge, imagination, and experience to work with our social leaders in an effort to turn the system around.

The task will unquestionably be a formidable one. Yet we have overcome formidable hurdles in the past, and doing so has made America great. The tools of success are at hand.

Business organizations effectively use the principles of management, control, and evaluation, and these principles are also available to government and social institutions. The proven strategies of business management, along with their natural off-shoots, work not only in the commercial sector, but have been applied successfully in scores of nonprofit programs.

Competitive intelligence makes it possible to determine ways and means of getting the jump on the competition in quality, productivity, and market acceptance.

Technology transfer, applied extensively in the aerospace in-dustry, formalizes the procedure of disseminating information throughout the enterprise so that multiple mileage can be achieved from outstanding capabilities, innovations, and ideas.

Management by objectives ties the planning and funding of programs and facilities to well-defined and clearly stated short- and long-term goals.

Profitability accounting is designed to identify wasteful and nonproductive elements in a system and root them out.

Incentive techniques provide individual recognition and make it personally rewarding to meet and exceed high stan-dards of performance while at the same time they see that me-diocrity and indifference are penalized.

The business management concepts underlying the ten basic principles of Socio-Economic Management, developed over the years and streamlined through the application of advanced management technology, have been mainly responsible for the unprecedented growth of our massive industrial complex. They have worked so well in business that the U.S. industrial sector, for all its imperfections, is used as a model of excellence throughout the entire civilized world.

Our social institutions, unfortunately, have lagged far behind. As American corporations grew in effectiveness and strength, the nonprofit institutions that serve society were also expanded. But these grew on a paste-up basis. One piece was added here, another there. An agency was set up in this place, a program in that, a commission or study group elsewhere.

Our social institutions swelled, but they grew only in size. Expansion was generated in a carbon copy pattern, the result of recording what was done in the past and planning more of the same for the future.

This might have been acceptable if what was done had

served our needs. But if there is one point that even the status-quoticians concede, it is that our needs have not been, and are not being, served. Indeed, they cannot be served until a service system is created.

Stockholders, directors, and executive superiors keep hammering away to the business manager to "show a profit" in his individual area of responsibility. The public manager, on the other hand, however beset by pressures and tensions, has never been compelled to justify his existence and performance in terms of social profitability or fulfilled human needs. Society can no longer afford this luxury of "benign neglect."

Our social institutions can be made effective only if we devise new approaches to the way they are designed, managed, and financed. We must identify and acknowledge those goal-directed segments of our social improvement efforts that are producing beneficial results for mankind. These we must continue and expand. At the same time, we must spotlight the programs and practices that squander public funds and retard progress. These we must stop, however great the jolt to entrenched bureaupolitocrats who seek only to perpetuate their hierarchies.

We have at our disposal the manpower, brainpower, and technological capability to properly generate, monitor, report, and continually refine our tax-supported services. All we need is the will. Through the rational systems approach I have labeled Socio-Economic Management, we can redesign the non-profit sector so that it will be responsive to human requirements and held accountable for results. Using SEM as our framework for restructuring, we can solve the problems of our cities and streets as successfully as we are solving the problems of our offices and plants. To do so, we must break away from the "law of government administration" that says the less productive a program administrator, the more money he gets to expand operations.

WHO WILL DO THE JOB?

So who's elected? Quite frankly, you and I are elected, every one of us—businessman, professional, government official, agency head, and private citizen alike—who has a stake in this nation's survival.

Common Cause has made a fervent appeal to all concerned Americans to form a new, independent, nonpartisan organization to help in the rebuilding of the most wonderful country ever formed on this earth. SEM makes a similar appeal.

In these crucial times we can no longer afford to abdicate our responsibility for survival by leaving social reform to those individuals whose job descriptions presumably qualify them for the job. We can no longer afford to confine our concern to lamentations about stifling bureaucracies and ambitious politicians.

The time is long overdue for every concerned American to put his time and money where it really counts to help initiate change, and to end the status quo. If enough of us get together to work toward this end, the giant "tug of peace" will not end in civil war.

2

SURVIVAL RECIPE: SOCIO-ECONOMIC MANAGEMENT

An endless variety of questions confront those who try to answer today's social and economic problems. These are just some of them:

Are we responding to the needs of the disadvantaged in their proper order of priority?

How much money should we put into the hiring and training of more policemen to combat crime on the streets? And how much into programs to control drug use and improve the attitude of ghetto residents?

What part of the nation's health care investment should be used to qualify more doctors and build more hospitals? How much should be spent to improve the nation's health through dealing with such problems as smoking, drinking, and drug use?

Even if we had an abundance of physicians, how could we induce them to practice in dangerous and depressing slum areas? And if we fund massive programs to train and develop ghetto ethnocrats to assume leadership roles, how do we keep them in the ghetto once they're trained?

What about welfare? Do we relieve poverty more effectively by increasing the payments? Or do we get more mileage out of training programs designed to qualify the unemployables?

Such questions could be posed ad infinitum. And arguments in behalf of alternatives are as voluminous as the questions. Intelligent debate always has been an essential ingredient of progress and growth.

What is depressing is the discrepancy between the verbal responses and the social action needed to convert the rhetoric into simple acts of needs fulfillment. It is obvious, judging from scores of failures from Watts to Attica, involving everything from health care and transportation to employment and welfare, that the answers we're getting aren't meeting our national goals—goals we all too often haven't even bothered to define.

LIFELINE FROM INDUSTRY

Institution administrators and government officials aren't the only ones who must cope with harrowing questions, perplexing alternatives, agonizing decisions. Business executives have been facing them for years—and coming up with much better results. Not because they're smarter, more talented, more dedicated, more imaginative, or more of anything else than social managers. They're coming up with successful solutions because they have no other choice.

When a company invests substantial resources in a major endeavor and flops, at best it is badly crippled, at worst it goes under. Not so the average social agency. Here, dubious programs are too often perpetuated. Where failure is blatantly apparent, the program is discontinued and a new one set up. One rarely hears of a welfare agency going out of business because it's not doing well, or of a hospital administrator, university president, or poverty program director losing his job due to lackluster performance. But the business press is full of stories about companies spun off, plants shut down, top executives replaced because objectives aren't met.

The imperatives are clear. And because of the imperatives, every management tool available is applied to problems, programs, and decisions in an effort to optimize the chances for success. This is in striking contrast to the nontools that are used by most social agencies.

Still, the prospects for the future are not all that bleak. In particular, there are heartening similarities between managing a business and managing a social agency. Very often the same kind of analysis and value judgment are applicable in tackling problems and formulating decisions. Both social and business managers must allocate manpower and financial and physical resources in the most effective manner possible.

Take a hypothetical well-run company, National Consumer Products, Inc. Its objective is profit improvement and corporate growth. (The social equivalent—or social profitability—would be needs fulfillment.) To achieve its goals, National might embark on a variety of programs: plant expansion, acquisition, product line enlargement, new market penetration.

Which route to choose can be a harrowing decision. Endless questions relating to each alternative would be posed, factors and subfactors weighed, changing conditions assessed. Suppose in the end a decision for new market penetration is made. It could never be foolproof, but one thing is certain: Every available management strategy would have been applied to test that decision before it was implemented, while it was being implemented, and when the results were coming in.

Management is the operational word. Not haphazard. Not hit-or-miss.

A business venture, like an experimental social program, cannot be risk-free. There's no guarantee that market penetration will fulfill expectations, or even succeed. But abundant evidence exists that a given business venture has more chance of succeeding than a given social venture. This is simply because it is standard business practice to minimize risk by applying the total management approach to the funding and evaluation of projects and programs.

Nothing could be more practical. During recent decades, vast mountains of manpower, money, and expertise have been invested in developing sophisticated management strategies that run the gamut from interdisciplinary planning, goal setting, standards, and measurement to profitability accounting, value analysis, and management by objectives. These strategies are working today for thousands of well-run companies. And they're not restricted to the industrial marketplace. They're as applicable to the social institution as they are to the commercial enterprise.

The application of Socio-Economic Management for social institutions could start today. Zeroed in on needs fulfillment, it would pinpoint "profitable" programs and reject endeavors that are economically, functionally, or humanly impractical. Most important, starting now it could supplement the rhetoric and debate with results-oriented action.

SEM: THE CONCEPT AND APPROACH

Socio-Economic Management is the logical extension of socio-economic accounting—the measurement and analysis of the social and economic consequences of governmental and business actions on the public sector. It gives the lie to the commonly accepted government-appropriations syndrome that spending money is synonymous with doing the job.

The no-other-choice imperative compels businessmen to focus regularly and repeatedly on the bottom line of the profit-and-loss statement. Social institutions have never been concerned with this net profit figure or its equivalent. To the agency administrator and program director, it does not even exist. Here is an important reason why commercial enterprise has been more successful than social enterprise.

The chief purpose—no longer the *only* purpose—for which a corporation is created is to produce income for its stockholders. If it fails in this purpose it does not remain in business.

The chief purpose—the *only* purpose—for which a social agency is created is to meet human needs. The reason these needs so often remain unfulfilled is that institutions have never been required to justify their existence by "showing a profit." A social organization can increase in size, in unwieldiness, in inefficiency, and still remain in business.

Socio-Economic Management is based on the premise that it makes little difference whether profit performance is gauged in terms of dollars earned or human needs met. To sustain the profitability of any enterprise, commercial or social, measurement standards and effective measurement techniques are essential. Only through such techniques can an organization's existence be justified or a program's effectiveness assessed.

Socio-Economic Management, by means of its proven system of guidelines, evaluation strategies, and controls, puts social profitability on a par with business profitability. The following ten basic management rules have been set forth in an effort to bring new efficiency to this nation's social institutions and to halt much of the squandering of public funds. The rules themselves are not new, but their application to social institutions is new.

THE TEN RULES OF SOCIO-ECONOMIC MANAGEMENT

Rule 1. Tie standards and goals to proven human needs

It is not possible to set needs-related goals and evaluate results properly without applying qualitative standards of performance to social endeavors. In recent decades we have become a society of counters, playing down life values and playing up the numbers game. We are well-equipped to develop numerical data, but ill-equipped to come up with meaningful answers that relate to the quality of life.

We know how many housing units are built to replace slum dwellings, but we don't know if the slum-dweller's well-being has been improved. We know what our prison population is, but we don't know how many prisoners are being rehabilitated. We measure the number of policemen on the force, but not how safe our streets are. We pour billions each year into a Department of Health, Education, and Welfare and an Office of Education. But we don't try to determine how well our young people are being educated. The objectives of our social institutions are vague, and our national goals are so distorted that we fund $21,600 to kill an enemy soldier in Vietnam, but only $6.27 per patient for heart-disease research.

There's no need at this stage in our country's development to operate under quantitative standards alone. Yet while qualitative standards are available, they are not being used. Transportation problems in the military, for example, are tackled with the most modern management tools available, but in domestic transportation, with millions of commuters involved, no similar effort has been made.

The standards are there. Educators and sociologists are able to determine the level of reading, writing, or arithmetic proficiency achieved by a youngster, as well as his level of social development. Penologists have standards for ascertaining when a former prisoner has been rehabilitated. And in recent years the trend toward qualitative standards has been growing in business.

Research and development programs are qualitatively tested to determine the number and importance of products developed. The sophisticated business analyst applies qualitative evaluation to operating results. He refers to "quality of earnings"—that is, consistent and predictable income as opposed to earnings that are variable and uncertain. Price-earnings ratios are another form of qualitative measure. Market studies measure not only the increased volume from a sales campaign, but the number of repeat orders as well.

It is interesting to note that Police Commissioner Patrick V. Murphy of New York stated recently: "Increasing the number of policemen does not prevent crime. We do not even know what causes crime. We do not know why people commit crime." Yet the efficiency of police departments is measured by the number of criminals apprehended, and their budgets are directly related to the number of personnel on the staff, without consideration for whether the causes of crime are even being identified and attacked.

The scientific management techniques of goal and standard setting could change this. The cost-effectiveness approach, which works so well for thousands of corporations, forces management to think through objectives and standards and to link them to proven needs. There is evidence indicating that such techniques can, with some modification, work for social institutions as well.

Rule 2. Apply funding by results

We pour billions of dollars each year into social programs. Presumably such programs are designed to meet the crucial needs of our citizens.

We pour billions into education.

In a little over 20 years, America's public education budget increased 1,000 percent—from about $6.5 billion in 1947 to $68 billion in 1969. A distinguished educator, Dr. Leon Lessenger, tells us that if costs continue to climb as they have in the past, spending on education would eventually equal the entire gross national product.

How effectively are the funds applied? A study recently conducted under the auspices of the Carnegie Commission on Higher Education charges that higher education, as one example, is being operated as a handicraft industry—basically unaffected by technological advances and automation. Productivity, it claims, has not kept pace with the rate of productivity improvement elsewhere in the nation, and in industry particularly.

We pour billions into transportation.

The city of Los Angeles is spending $200 million to buy up some 2,000 houses of inhabitants made desperate by jet planes using the nearby municipal airport. "The victims are to be congratulated on their release from a tortured existence," comments a *New York Times* editorial writer, "but what is to be said for the reasoning processes of a society that can waste money at that rate which might more readily have been used to soften the noises of jet planes to the point of making them endurable?"

We pour billions into welfare.

Welfare is currently costing the state of California about $3 billion a year. In ten years its rolls have swelled from 620,000 to 2.4 million. At this writing one out of nine persons in California is on some kind of welfare. Governor Ronald Reagan fears that if something isn't done in a hurry, it will soon be one out of seven. It is apparent that the billions being funded do not serve to decrease the client population, which is another way of saying that human needs are not being met.

We pour additional billions into housing, crime control, job programs, health care, drug treatment, recreation, and the environment. The dollars pyramid, but the problems don't shrink. There is obviously something wrong with the way our financial resources are being allocated. Just as obviously, we are funding social programs not by results, but by the numbers, by political expediency, and by guesswork.

Before we fund by results, we must first establish how to measure and evaluate results. After pinpointing needs and setting objectives, we must be able to ascertain how well a program is doing. Is it fulfilling its purpose? Has productivity improved over the past year? How close to projected results did actual performance come? How well is Program A doing compared with Program B?

Such answers aren't easy to come by. But similar problems arise in business, and the methodology—profitability accounting, for example—has been developed to solve them. The evidence indicates that the methodology is applicable to social institutions as well.

Rule 3. Use discretionary funding as incentives

When business managers succeed, they receive cash bonuses, stock options, and the like as incentives to continued excellence and even greater achievement. The motivation works because business executives are known to respond to material stimulation.

Managers of nonprofit organizations require a different kind of motivation. The social administrator pursues his profession largely because his main concern is with teaching the young, alleviating the plight of the poor, rehabilitating criminals, caring for the sick and the aged. He is more interested in improving the quality of life in America than in accumulating material assets. If this weren't so, he'd seek a business career.

The motivation that works best for managers of social programs is discretionary funding—making money available for use at the manager's discretion as a reward for innovation, experimentation, and the development and expansion of pet projects. To the creative teacher, the dedicated welfare worker, the concerned penologist, and the hospital administrator, the prospect of such funds can be a heady and inspiring incentive.

Yet realistically, however dedicated these men and women may be, they cannot be oblivious to material needs. Outstanding performance under incentive arrangements would solve this problem as well. Increased responsibility and organizational expansion are automatic byproducts of excellence. With growth comes added status and personal and financial recognition. Thus, discretionary funding and other incentives would serve on the one hand as a powerful stimulant to improved social profitability, and on the other as a disincentive to penalize mediocrity.

Rule 4. Use multidisciplinary planning

No corporate chief executive would unilaterally decide to embark on an expansion program. He would first consult with his marketing, manufacturing, financial, and engineering people. He would trade ideas with investment executives, industry specialists, accountants, bankers, economists, management consultants. In short, he would bring a variety of professional disciplines to bear on the problems involved. He would take advantage of all the experience and expertise at his disposal in evaluating and resolving the elements that bear on the decision.

Social programs and problems are infinitely more complex than their business counterparts. In addition, vast sums of money are involved. Yet all too often we see sociologists, economists, and statisticians performing accounting functions without an adequate understanding of accounting principles and concepts, or of budgetary procedures and managerial controls. We see administrators of health, correctional, educational, and welfare institutions performing management tasks for which they possess neither the background nor the training. The results are predictable. If you hire even the most skilled and talented dentist in the world to build a tunnel, it would be wishful thinking to expect sound construction.

As Mancur Olson, Jr., a former deputy assistant secretary of HEW, has pointed out: "The various disciplines are distinguished by their prejudices and their methods. . . . Since different disciplines sometimes lead to different conclusions about the same problem, we must hope for more communication and debate among the different social science [and business management] disciplines, and deplore the parochialism which is, alas, at its worst in my own field."

Case histories are in evidence, and some will be cited in this book, which prove the efficacy of adding varied disciplines, including professional capabilities in business management and accounting, to skills currently being utilized in the field of nonprofit enterprise. Management activists on the policy-making level are urgently needed to augment the efforts of theoreticians and social planners. The techniques of business executives include defining objectives, setting standards, getting projects started on schedule, and moving them along. The techniques of accountants, who are society's measurement experts, include evaluating results and tying them to objectives, setting up budgets, and establishing controls.

The poor must also play a major role in program planning and evaluation if real needs are to be properly addressed and met. Dramatic proof of this was hammered home in one New England city where a massive and expensive effort was made to alleviate outrageous conditions in a ghetto community. Without anyone consulting the disadvantaged recipients of the program or their representatives, a variety of housing, training, and recreational "improvements" were made. Only when the citizens complained bitterly about these gratuitous undertakings were they brought into the picture.

"What else can we give you?" they were asked. "What more do you want?"

The answer was dogs. The sociologists and other experts were astounded. "Dogs!" It didn't make sense. But it made all the sense in the world to the members of that community whose buildings were infested and overrun by rats. Rats endangered their health and the lives of their babies. As far as they were concerned, rat control was the number one priority—above playgrounds, above better bus service, above job training.

In social enterprise, as in business, a variety of skills, viewpoints, and philosophies must be applied to a problem before a plan can be structured to resolve it. Omit even one of these crucial links—be it managerial, sociological, or accounting control —and you invite trouble.

There is no longer any need or rational excuse for omission. The effectiveness of multidisciplinary coordination has long been established.

Rule 5. Set up social profitability audits
When billions of dollars of public funds are invested in social programs, the public and its elected representatives are entitled to a qualitative evaluation of how the funds are being spent.

Are objectives properly geared to the fulfillment of human needs? Have meaningful standards been set up to insure that the goals will be met? Are intermediate goals being reached on schedule?

We must cease to concentrate on short-term emergency measures while ignoring the long-term solutions. When dealing with people living in poverty, we cannot underrate the importance of food today, clothing today, shelter today. But this should not be the end objective of a poverty program. When we give a man a fish we feed him for a day. But this isn't enough. We must teach him how to fish so he can feed himself for the rest of his life. If we give the drug addict a fix or the alcoholic a drink, it may serve his short-term need. But to do him any good over the long range and to help society, we must teach him how to kick his habit.

The poverty or drug program, to be ideally effective, must seek to put itself out of business, to be left without clients. Yet the administrator who helps meet this goal would not excel himself out of a job, but would be the most sought-after professional in his field.

The day of the college administrator who focuses primarily on ways of processing the maximum number of students and grinding out the maximum number of degrees is drawing to an end. Tomorrow's successful educator will be more concerned with the best mix of resources for preparing students for a better life and a more meaningful contribution to society.

Financial audits are accepted and effectively used in all sectors of activity—business, government, nonprofit. Also, many of these same organizations use management audits to examine the efficiency with which the various functions are being executed. Now we need socio-economic audits for our social institutions to determine whether the resources put into a program are directed toward the true objectives of the program.

Regular socio-economic auditing should be put into widespread local and national use to keep the public informed and to serve as a guideline for officials with budgetary responsibility for the allocation of public resources. How to do this will be covered in a later chapter.

Rule 6. Establish public visibility

Mr. Califano: In late 1968 I asked the appropriate government agencies how the 10 million figure (10 million hungry persons) was developed. . . . I was told by the then Secretary of Health,

Education, and Welfare that what they had done was to take a rough estimate of the number of people who were poor, figured about 2 million of the adults were actually hungry, multiplied that by 4½ to get a family figure, and that is where they got 10 million people.
Senator Mondale: It was just a complete guess, wasn't it?
Mr. Califano: That is correct.

That exchange has been excerpted from testimony given at a Senate subcommittee hearing in 1969. It is a shocking indication of the way vital social information is developed in this nation and made known to the public.

An assistant secretary of HEW told a congressional subcommittee: "We simply do not know whether children who received medical checkups and continuous medical attention are healthier than those who do not."

We should have such information. The public should have it. Elected officials, budgetary authorities, boards of trustees, and the social administrators themselves should have it. If it is lacking, how can we properly appropriate billions of dollars of the public's money for hunger relief, health care, education, crime control, and all the rest?

In the well-run corporation, performance is evaluated and reported on a regular basis. Managers are rewarded or penalized on the basis of it. Programs are initiated, expanded, or cut back as reported results and reported potential dictate. No president would seriously consider enlarging a plant, expanding a product line, launching a sales campaign, making an acquistion, or planning financial strategy without business reporting to guide him.

"How are we doing?" The question is posed repeatedly in the modern business establishment. Day after day. Week after week. And performance reports provide the answers. Too often the answers are unprovided on the social scene.

How many welfare recipients are being made self-sufficient? How many children's reading skills are being boosted to an acceptable level? How many ex-convicts are being employed in socially acceptable jobs?

We simply don't know. We do not know if the lot of the disadvantaged is being improved at a rate sufficient to counteract the desperation and frustration that impel men to riot.

Yet numbers are only data. They're not necessarily information. They're not always intelligence. As far as funding is concerned, they quite often may be misleading.

How are we doing? There lies the key. How much are we alleviating hardship and poverty? To what degree are we improving public safety? How effectively are we responding to the nation's housing needs?

A system of social reporting similar to our system of economic reporting would reply to such questions with qualitative answers. Our economic indicators and reports, while far from perfect, have been highly effective in helping to plan economic strategy. Professional planners can get a fairly accurate fix on national income, inflation, recession, interest rates, hourly wages, prices, and unemployment.

Scores of social reformers in and out of government strongly believe that economic reports no longer suffice. Social reports are needed to accompany and supplement them at all levels of social enterprise from the federal government to the rural township. Social progress—or a lack of it—should be made known to the public and the press.

Social institutions that exist only to serve the public should certainly respond to this need for fuller reporting. Their response is long overdue.

Rule 7. Prune and restructure for dynamic growth

It happens every day in business. Two small companies are individually unable to afford the marketing, tooling, or research programs they need to achieve profit objectives. So they merge and thereby consolidate their resources.

A few years ago technologically powerful North American Aviation Co. found itself lacking marketing muscle. About the same time market-savvy Rockwell Standard Corp. became concerned over shortcomings in its technical capability. So the companies merged, creating an entity that was strong in both marketing and technology.

When Walter Kidde & Co. discovered that its acquired division, United States Lines, was improperly suited to its mix of products and management talents, the holding was sold to R. J. Reynolds Industries, where the match was much better. When the recently appointed head of General Motors' Chevrolet Motor Division, John Z. DeLorean, sought to turn around Chevy's declining profit performance, one of his first moves was an overhaul of the organization structure. In manufacturing, says DeLorean, "we actually eliminated three levels of management between the plant manager and the general manufacturing manager."

Endless pages could be filled with stories of business pruning, merger, and restructuring. It would take very little space to document similar activity in the nonprofit sector, where it is needed so much more urgently.

Obsolete, oppressive, and sometimes corrupt organizations exist all around us. Because the proven management tools of restructuring are only rarely put to use, today's despotism in our society is one of institution versus man.

Proof is not hard to come by. A recently published survey by the Morgan Guaranty Trust Company of New York reveals that in the past decade government employment at all levels, excluding the armed forces, has grown by 51 percent, compared with a 19 percent rise in the total labor force. If things go on like that, the bank said, every American will be working for the government by 2049—a century and a half sooner than in Britain.

It has been further disclosed that the federal government spends $75 million a year to support 2,200 advisory committees. A House probe found many of these committees were meaningless, obsolete, or performing duplicate jobs. A Marine Corps memorial commission, for example, created in 1947 to consider plans for a monument in Chicago, had done little or nothing in the 23 years it had existed up to the time the probe was undertaken.

We see evidence of gross overorganization in every field of social endeavor. It is produced by confused objectives, overlapping functions, sinecures clung to that should have been abolished long ago. We see innumerable institutions, departments, and committees that have outlived their usefulness, but continue to exist. New activities are undertaken, new organization superimposed on the old. The resulting nonorganization is chaotic. When an agency loses sight of its true objectives, deterioration is inevitable. It becomes clogged with needless forms and labyrinthine procedures. Efficiency suffers, effectiveness wanes.

The need for serious social restructuring is critical, and not at some vague future date, but today. To cite one of many examples, the Bureau of Reclamation, the Corps of Engineers, and the Soil Conservation Service are all involved in water development programs. Their projects often overlap. They work at cross-purposes. While costs escalate, progress is hindered through lack of coordination and cooperation.

Proponents of more efficient law enforcement have long urged a broader regional approach, one that would permit police to cross local jurisdictional lines in the solution of crimes and the apprehension of criminals. The wide range of criminal activity in such areas has small respect for political boundaries. But we see little action stirring along these lines.

The social improvement potential of organizational restructuring is exciting. Here and there we see breakthroughs taking place. In the Washington, D.C. area a pact was signed to restructure law enforcement in an effort to de-rigidify local dominions. It falls short of the need, but it's a start.

In Arizona, eight hospitals were combined into the Samaritan Health Service. They ranged in size from 14 to 724 beds. Their merger not only considerably strengthened their financial base but improved their utilization of professional services and technical facilities. The economies were enormous, including a first-year saving of $90,000 in insurance premiums alone. Similar health care consolidations have taken place elsewhere in the United States, with dramatic gains registered.

The benefits of merger, divestiture, pruning, and restructuring are well understood in the business community. These same approaches should be applied to social institutions and government agencies. The time for such action is ripe.

Rule 8. Vary the input mix

Business's major objective is profit improvement. Management's responsibility is to find the combination of input resources to produce the best financial results. This won't just happen. However scientifically management principles are applied, experimentation and innovation must play a vital role.

To come up with the winning combination, business managers try a variety of advertising and promotional strategies. They engage in research and development, testing new packaging and new methods of distribution. They experiment with raw materials, manufacturing processes, machine tools, motivational techniques. The businessman does not take profit for granted. He varies the input mix to continually improve earnings performance.

Social endeavors fall short in this area. Stultifying status quoism too often applies to programs and projects. Innovation is comparatively infrequent and when it does occur, usually meets with tough resistance.

Imagination is the taproot of improvement. Without it, there can be little progress. We must treat social programs as products with social values, and experiment with a variety of inputs to produce the best results.

When imaginative social management is applied, the prospects can be exciting and stimulating. In Boston, Technical Development Corporation, a nonprofit organization devoted to reforming criminal justice processes, is conducting an experiment called "pretrial intervention." The experiment, financed by the U.S. Department of Labor, has already worked successfully in Washington and New York. Pretrial intervention is designed to siphon off misdemeanor cases from clogged court dockets and give offenders who might otherwise land in jail a chance to redeem themselves through assignment to a rehabilitation team. The carefully screened offender returns to court after 90 days. If the signs are encouraging, the judge may decide to dismiss the charge, and rehabilitation continues after dismissal.

In California, Superintendent of Public Instruction Wilson Riles plans to start the state's 4½ million public school children a year before the present kindergarten age of five. The biggest gainers, Riles thinks, would be disadvantaged students and taxpayers. His reasoning: "Prevention is cheaper than remediation. A dollar spent on the very young goes farther than a dollar for the not-so-young who are in remedial classes or on welfare or, indeed, on the 'wanted' bulletins of post office walls." It is a proposal of such staggering simplicity, *Time* magazine observes, that it is already meeting opposition.

Riverton, a proposed "new town" near Rochester, New York, plans to feature a services barter program. This will enable people to trade services instead of money for things they need so that all income groups can afford the amenities of the community.

It is clear that more such imaginative thinking is needed in our struggle for social improvement. And so much more is possible, and fundable. Why can't we, for example, in an attempt to relieve poverty, set up kibbutz-type communities in the inner city, or in one large building, or in the nearby countryside? Here, inhabitants could learn to live and work together and respond to the challenge of maintaining clean and healthful surroundings. Perhaps they could even produce a product for sale in the marketplace.

Why not apply some poverty-input resources to establish trade training centers in ghetto districts? Such centers could at the same time be government-supported industry, owned and operated by ghetto residents. The ventures could be temporarily subsidized to compete effectively with established plants. In time, if successful, they would stand on their own and fulfill the ultimate in social profitability—the elimination of human needs by helping disadvantaged citizens to help themselves.

Rule 9. Stir up social competition
Business is subjected to a measuring rod that is ruthlessly applied—that of the marketplace. The marketplace determines whether a business organization shall live or die. If a company fails to maintain high standards, it will be deserted by its customers. In time it will fold.

There exists no equivalent for the outputs of social institutions, no competitive pressures for excellence. The ghetto clients of poverty programs have little if any effect on whether or not a program is expanded or discontinued. This is decided by officials who base their decisions on numbers, on what was done last year and the year before, on a perpetuation of the status quo.

We need marketplace mechanisms and a greater number of competitive options for our social institutions. In too many city core areas, and in health care particularly, only one institution is accessible to disadvantaged clients. Whether this institution is run inefficiently or not, it is the only place they can turn for help. No wonder there is so much frustration.

We need a multiplex of programs and facilities for the poor —alternative clinics and hospitals, private and public practitioners, dental care centers that compete against each other for the health care dollar and so are forced to maintain high standards if they are to flourish and survive. We need health care insurance options that would give society the most for its inputs.

The opportunities for providing and expanding the kind of choice that breeds excellence extend as far as the imagination of innovative managers and public officials. We could incorporate into our welfare program, for example, an option that offers the client a choice between $100 in welfare money on the one hand and $200 worth of industrial training on the other. The avowed purpose of prisons is not incarceration, but rehabilitation. Why not set up different types of rehabilitation institutions and permit prisoners to select the kind of institution that appeals to them most strongly and that presumably would have the greatest motivational effect?

No intelligent observer of today's social scene would pretend that the options we need are devoid of problems, or easy to apply. But the road ahead is clear. Desperation is high and patience is low. The options exist whether we want them or not. How much better to install them voluntarily in an intelligently planned manner than on a crash basis generated by fear.

Rule 10. Fix responsibility for applying SEM
The number of plans that have been proposed to cure this nation's social ills could probably stock a good-size library. Why should Socio-Economic Management succeed where others have failed? What is needed to help transform this particular blueprint from paper to reality?

The functional key is responsibility—public responsibility, private responsibility, administrative responsibility. By whatever label we choose to call it, more effective management of our social institutions is on the way. Whether they evolve peacefully or painfully, change and reform are inevitable. Businessmen know it. The public knows it. Institution heads know it. Elected officials know it.

SEM has the most powerful ally in a democratic society on its side—the vote. Politicians are adept at reading the signs. Whether motivated by conscience or the desire to remain in office, or both, elected officials from Washington, D.C. to Twin Falls, Montana will respond.

Senator Mondale has long pioneered for legislation to create a Council of Social Advisers to develop "social indicators" and report the state of our social health to the nation.

Proceeding a step further, Socio-Economic Management Councils (SECs) could be created at every level of government. Multidisciplinary in nature, they would analyze existing social programs to determine the extent to which valid objectives are being met.

A local SEC might be established to attack the mugging problem in a ghetto area. Educators, psychologists, criminologists, and sociologists would interpret behavioral and criminal tendencies. Crime sources and causes would be rooted out. Recommendations would be made, programs formulated. Business executives would help to get the action going. Accountants would be enlisted to monitor progress and measure results.

Apart from this, the basic rules of SEM could be applied at once in government agencies and nonprofit institutions.

3

HUMAN NEEDS:
THE
LAUNCHING PAD

A pet story of Allyn Robinson, president of Dowling College, is the one about the pastor who visited a sick congregant in the hospital. The man was in an oxygen tent and unable to speak, so the pastor got out his Bible and began reading psalms to him. During the reading, the sick man began to stir restlessly, then reached for a nearby pencil and pad and began to write.

Though the pastor considered this rather rude, he tolerantly continued to read. In time he observed that the man's face was looking pained and turning red. Concerned, the pastor rang for the nurse, who checked the patient and informed the pastor he had died. As the body was being wheeled from the room, the pastor saw the notepad lying on the dead man's chest and glanced over to read it.

"Pastor, please," the note said, "you are standing on my oxygen tube."

Too many social organizations today are standing on the oxygen tubes of people they're supposed to be aiding, thereby destroying initiative, undermining hope and creativity, and in extreme cases inciting to riot. Presumably we have formed a social order for the purpose of fulfilling human needs. There is no other justification for publicly funded organizations to exist.

Yet we continue to deal with needs in traditional and obsolete terms. Based on superficial conclusions, insufficient evidence, and political expediency, we give people what we think they should have instead of what they really require. We urgently need a change in social values so that our goals are changed from increasing the quantity of production to improving the quality of life. Most of our society and its institutions are geared to material growth. The sooner we begin to think in terms of changing from quantity to quality as our primary social purpose, the less difficult will be the task of fulfillment.

NARROWING THE INTELLIGENCE GAP

If the launching pad for social turnaround in America is human needs, the fuel for the blast-off is research and analysis. Despite the millions being spent on innumerable studies and probes, we fall pitifully short in this area.

Richard Ruggles, a Yale University economist, maintains that the present form of accounting used by government cannot readily encompass related social and demographic information. For example, it is not possible to study problems of poverty and discrimination in the context of the data provided in existing national accounts. Despite the technological revolution in processing and handling produced by the computer, this factor is not reflected in the design or use of our economic accounting system.

We still fund by the numbers. Budget officials and agency administrators tend to categorize population segments as "better off" when programmed doles are expanded, "worse off" when they're not.

We thus perpetuate the quantification of human needs in terms of existing output, existing programs, existing agencies. Yet in most areas of social endeavor we are unable to measure with a practical degree of assurance the adequacy of what we are doing or what we have done. Only from the feedback of impassioned protest can we derive any feel at all for the amount of corrective headway being made or determine how much social coolant must be applied. The vehemence of protest has become a prime gauge of human dissatisfaction and program motivation in our time.

What we practice is decibel response. It is a reckless and grossly unfair system of disbursing public assets. Articulate social lobbies supported by labor, or the academic community, or powerful consumer advocates, for example, get the lion's share of the funding, often on a giveaway basis. Less vigorous lobbies, like that of the aged, or the disadvantaged Indian, get little more than lip service. (I must quickly add that as this manuscript is being prepared to go to press, it appears that the Indian lobby has begun to assert itself a bit more forcefully.) Surely we need a more scientific means than this of determining society's needs and assessing needs fulfillment.

The problem is of grave concern to all sectors of the non-profit community. Our social institutions desperately need the businessman's pragmatic, profit-minded approach to program development and expansion. In the profitable corporation, intensive market research, with return on investment in mind, would precede any major marketing campaign. Intensive site location research would precede the establishment of a new distribution center or plant.

Why not intensive needs-directed research and analysis to determine which programs we should initiate, which we should expand, which we should abandon—with social return on investment, the clear identification of needs, in mind?

Any other course can only increase present waste. Attempting to satisfy human needs without first identifying them accurately is like attempting to deliver a package without knowing the address. But there is no reason for the address to remain a mystery. To repeat: We do possess the know-how and experience to conduct the research and assess the results. We possess the tools and technology. We have only to use them.

The need for their use is apparent. We rarely see research and analytical capabilities in evidence in public agencies and institutions. For example, the most basic information regarding welfare recipients—who they are, how many are able-bodied, what quality-of-life improvement, if any, is achieved from the doles—is difficult if not impossible to come by in most U.S. cities and on the federal level.

PRODUCT ACCEPTANCE

Suppose a large corporation found itself faced with serious problems of product acceptance. What would it do? There's little doubt that the president, directors, and high level executives would have to pose some searching questions regarding the manner in which the company was identifying, addressing itself to, and fulfilling customer needs. Is the product doing what it was designed to do? Is its quality being sustained? Is service living up to expectations and commitments?

It would address these questions and others to customers and salesmen, supervisors and managers. When it came up with the answers, they would be carefully studied and analyzed. Finally, in the light of what was learned, major reforms would be made. Either that, or the company would go out of business.

An alarmingly high number of this nation's nonprofit organizations are faced with critical problems of product acceptance. An outstanding example is the American system of "corrective rehabilitation," our network of prisons. These organizations are charged with reforming lawbreakers and returning them as productive citizens to the mainstream of life. Whichever way you look at it, "product acceptance" in these institutions is at a dangerously low level.

If you regard the inmates as the products of our corrective institutions, they are quite obviously unacceptable to the society called upon to receive them when their penance is done, or indeed to themselves after being processed through the system. As Russell G. Oswald, New York State corrections commissioner, has expressed it: "Our job somehow is to motivate for change inside these institutions. . . . As we change our thinking about our institutions, we must realize that the vast majority in prisons are crying out for help. They want the opportunity for change. But the way it is now, our security is geared to the troublemakers. That means about 200 people in a prison population of 1,800 need maximum security, so we must have it for the entire group."

In 1967, President Johnson's National Crime Commission reported that of the half billion dollars funded annually for prisons, 95 cents out of each dollar was earmarked for custody, only a nickel for correction. There's little evidence to show that the situation has been appreciably altered in the years since.

American prisons continue to be run as lock vaults for society's bad pennies. We degrade, brutalize, and dehumanize inmates and then label the procedure "corrective." Corrective indeed! The only prison I know of that has been aptly named is The Tombs.

Is it any wonder that prisoner uprisings have multiplied in recent years? New York's Attica Prison is simply one of the more chilling examples in view of the mayhem, bloodletting, and brutality that took place. There is some disagreement regarding what triggered the revolt on that September morning in 1971, but the nature of that incident does not matter. What does matter is that the tensions and frustrations were months in the building in Attica, as in other prisons from coast to coast. The conditions causing the revolt were as clear to government and prison officials as they were to the inmates.

Tom Wicker of *The New York Times* described the horrendous zoo with shudder-evoking lucidity:

The physical aspect of a place like Attica—the grim walls, the bare yards, the clanging steel—bespeaks the attitude that prisoners are wild animals to be caged. . . . Attica—like most prisons—is not a "correctional facility" at all; the phrase is a gruesome euphemism. No "correctional officer" there has any real training in correcting or teaching or counseling men; rather they are armed guards set to herd animals. Senselessly, every guard at Attica is white, save one reported Puerto Rican no observer ever saw; but the prisoners are 75 percent, or maybe 85 percent—no one seems to know for sure—black and Puerto Rican.

I have no desire to oversimplify the problems that exist in prisons. A minority of the inmates are chronic rapists, desperate drug addicts, perverts, and mindless killers. For such prisoners nothing short of maximum security rigidly enforced could protect the system itself and the society outside.

But the large majority of inmates demonstrably can be rehabilitated—given the guidance, concern, and respect they so desperately need. Does it make sense—whether one views the situation as a pragmatist or humanitarian—to sacrifice the majority in order to hogtie the few, thereby multiplying both criminals and crime?

The system is almost bankrupt, goes one argument; we can't afford the cost of rehabilitation. Such reasoning defies belief. It's like the businessman who maintains he can't afford to repair the damaged roof of his warehouse to prevent the water from leaking in and destroying his finished-goods inventory. Whatever the expense of attacking the problem in an intelligent and businesslike manner, it must be infinitesimal—from either an economic or humane standpoint—when compared with the cost of not attacking the problem.

Yet however desperate the situation, it is far from hopeless, and applying the principles of SEM will enable society to come up with viable solutions. But we must first lay the roadbed by identifying and examining all aspects of the problem and equipping ourselves with the information required to assign priorities and meet them successfully. We must ask the proper questions and invest in the necessary study to come up with the answers, just as any corporation would be forced to do if its survival were threatened.

What pressures cause crimes to be committed? What steps can we take to convert the bitterness and frustration of prisoners into feelings of faith and hope? How can dialogue and rapport between inmates and prison personnel be established? How can we motivate and equip prisoners for a productive life on the outside—and make society cooperative? And meanwhile, until turnaround takes place, what are the most effective methods for dealing with prison rebellion?

These questions and others must be answered. If we are to be judged on performance to date, we are patently blundering novices, both when it comes to easing prison tensions and returning inmates to the mainstream successfully. Experience proves that tightened security, while it restrains human bodies, cannot reform human minds. The man who thinks like a criminal will respond like a criminal. Why does he think the way he does? We don't know the answer at present. We know how to whip men into animal submission, but we can't give them hope.

Only through true objective-directed research and innovation based on its findings will other Atticas be prevented.

A TOO FAMILIAR PATTERN

The intelligence gap is apparent not only in dealing with crime, but in dealing with virtually all other social problems as well. As Professor René J. Dubos puts it: "We spend billions of dollars on building, but no one has studied what is the best size room for man to live in or work in. We have millions of children in classrooms with no windows just to save some money on broken glass and soot on the floor, but no one is studying what this does to the children."

In health care we see the pattern repeated. Little information is available, for example, on the state of children's health, although millions are proposed for various types of checkups and other clinic services. Estimates of degree of health improvement attributable to medical care are difficult to come by. And we have no way of knowing precisely how much healthier youngsters are who receive regular medical attention.

Relevant data upon which to predicate crucial decisions is of abiding concern to social planners and budget officials on all levels. Henry S. Rowen, former president of Rand Corporation, has noted both to me and before congressional committee hearings that we lack the means for tackling the problems effectively. At the federal level few departments have an analytic capacity of any consequence. They generally lack the ability to identify problems with precision, see that relevant data are collected, policy alternatives formulated, valid experiments run, existing programs evaluated. Rowen is convinced that the more complex question as to what is really being accomplished by these programs is rarely addressed in depth.

THE NEED FOR DISCLOSURE

When production lags in industry, orders fall off, defects mount above acceptable levels, customer complaints multiply, and all hell breaks loose. One of two actions follows: A management sleuth is rushed to the scene to investigate and report back to the chief, or the department head or division manager involved gets a curt note from the boss that demands in effect: "What the devil is happening?"

Periodic progress reporting these days is standard for every modern corporation whose aim is to remain in business. Special reporting is standard when established profit indicators stray off target. Disclosure, in short, is the corporate thread that keeps the performance fabric intact.

Disclosure prevents cover-ups by individuals who would prefer to conceal mediocrity. It gives successful programs the credit and recognition they deserve, pinpoints program flaws, spotlights actions that aren't paying their way.

However, meaningful reporting always has been and continues to be pitifully inadequate in social institutions in general and government agencies in particular.

"There is almost unanimous agreement," asserts Washington attorney and former government official Joseph A. Califano, Jr., "particularly among those who have tried to deal with our nation's social problems, that the tools of information, measurement, and evaluation, essential for intelligent programming, are virtually nonexistent in the government of the most technologically advanced nation in the history of mankind. . . . When one recognizes how costly are the honest mistakes that have been made in the Defense Department despite its sophisticated information systems, it becomes frightening to think of the mistakes which might be made on the domestic side of our government because of lack of adequate data."

Social indicators, regularly monitored and periodically reported, except on special occasions when serious deviations are flagged, could be set up to function in pretty much the same way profit indicators function in the modern corporation. Some typical indicators: calorie and protein consumption to evaluate nutritional level; density of occupancy for housing; access to hospitals and extent of preventive medicine for health care; level of reading, writing, and arithmetic proficiency for education; freedom to walk the streets at night; and safety in the home. Social indicators, in short, would be established to serve as the vehicles of disclosure.

Their value is self-evident. In the trouble-ridden city of Newark, New Jersey, for example, a 50-year-old dispensary was still operating in the spring of 1972 despite evidence that it had long since outlived its usefulness. A superior outpatient department in the more modern Martland Hospital nearby has for years been favored by the city's client population. According to a report issued in March 1972 by The Center for Analysis of

Public Issues, the number of patients treated at the decrepit facility dropped from 33,200 in 1966 to 5,900 in 1970. Despite this decrease, the report continues, the dispensary's budget jumped from $306,000 in 1966 to $500,000 in 1970.

When questioned about the accuracy of the report, Bailus Walker, Jr., director of Newark's Department of Health and Welfare, refutes these figures. He presents figures that are far less shocking, and attributes the discrepancy to a "newer procedure of keeping statistics, starting in 1969." But John M. Kolesar, the Center's director, states that the figures cited in the Center's report derive from the published budget for the City of Newark as approved by the City Council and from the 1970 Annual Report of the Division of Health. "If the Division developed 'a newer procedure for keeping statistics,' it was done after we concluded our research (December, 1971), for we rechecked all our data with Division officials before going to press."

Be that as it may. I have no desire to step into the midst of a squabble between Mr. Walker and Mr. Kolesar. Both men tried to be helpful and I have no doubt that both are sincere. In any case, the recommendation was made to close the dispensary and divert the half million dollars to the fulfillment of more pressing needs. In view of this city's desperate shortage of funds—let us assume that the Center's study was at least 50 percent accurate—the dispensary's perpetuation is a sad situation to behold.

What is more, taking into consideration the refutation and the counterrefutation, plus the confusion involved, what more eloquent argument could be posed for the need for a meaningful and reliable system of public disclosure in Newark and in all cities across the U.S.? If a system of disclosure had been put into operation a few years back, might not the folly and waste of continuing this apparently declining facility have been brought to light, a revelation that would have forced its shutdown? One can't help wondering.

As resources economist Nathaniel Wollman points out: "In order to generate public awareness, expert findings must be broadly disseminated. Occasionally environmental problems are dramatic enough to stimulate a spontaneous response, but more often they reflect, in [former Interior Secretary Stewart] Udall's phrase, a 'quiet crisis,' recognized by relatively few people. For this reason, a network of citizen groups is needed to serve as a link between the experts and the electorate."

Such groups, multidisciplinary in nature and properly authorized to follow up disclosures with corrective action, could act as vital agents of change and reform in our society.

The trend toward increased visibility for the actions taken by both public and private organizations continues to grow. Later, in suggesting specific steps we might take to implement the principles of Socio-Economic Management, I will discuss the concept of Socio-Economic Operating Statements (SEOS), a visibility vehicle for corporate enterprise designed to supplement the balance sheet and earnings statements on a periodic basis.

In providing a wider window on such nonprofit institutions as hospitals, prisons, and federal and local government agencies, the monitoring keys would be the social, or level-of-living, indicators already espoused by many sociologists and administrators and vigorously endorsed by Senator Mondale and other government officials. These will subsequently be described in more detail. But briefly, at this point, they could be set up to operate in pretty much the same way business indicators work in the "early warning systems" already installed in scores of modern U.S. operations.

In crime control, for example, we might apply police response time as one of several indicators to gauge police effectiveness. Or we might take the number of dead fish to monitor progress in reducing stream pollution. And so on down the line.

REPORTS, REPORTS, REPORTS

Out of Watts, out of Attica, out of Newark, Detroit, Pittsburgh, and every other riot-torn section of America we hear from bitter and disenchanted representatives of oppressed and hope-shorn minorities a common cry: "If there's one thing we don't need it's another report!"

The sentiment is as understandable as it is justified. In the past decade enough studies, reports, and reports on reports have been produced by special committees, task forces, and study groups to fill a good-sized office building. Despite this profusion of analyses documenting our social ills and the rec- ommended solutions accompanying them, conditions in most cases are essentially the same if not worse than before. So it is not surprising that when cries of despair from our ghettos are met with promises of "further study," the sick, the untrained, the jobless poor see red and view the proposal as yet another stall, another of Whitey's cooling strategies.

Still, the intelligence gap persists. It widens every day. We desperately need more answers—but answers from the true marketplace—and to communicate the answers we need mean- ingful reports. The alternative is to continue funding massive programs and manning mammoth organizations on the basis of political expediency and obsolete yes-man, guess-man random- ology. However distasteful the research route may seem—and it is distasteful only when it's misdirected—it makes more sense than playing pin-the-tail-on-the-donkey with our precious resources.

How much evidence do we require to be convinced that we are neither identifying nor responding to real human needs with any degree of effectiveness? Or that we are squandering our fast-shrinking financial resources in a miasma of uncertainty and confusion?

Traditionally, the largest single item in most big city budgets is education. In New York City recently, this long-standing tra- dition was broken. For the first time in history it is costing the city more to give its inhabitants handouts than it costs to give them knowledge. Over a million citizens are now on welfare, a jump of more than 200 percent over the 1960 figure.

This might be fine, even laudable, if the giveaway program made people happier or improved their standard of living in some discernible way. But, along with the booming relief rolls, we witness more crime and drug addiction, more family disrup- tion, more misery and frustration than ever before. We see little if any real upgrading in the level of life attributable to New York's all-time-record giveaway binge. And this holds true in city after city across the United States.

Poor people must be helped, of course. Failing to recognize this would be as economically unsound as it would be inhumane. But when the help that they receive worsens their condition instead of improving it—and when we cannot say why this is happening—is it not fair to assume the information we are acting upon is inadequate?

The solution is as clear as the problem. We will not come up with better ways to alleviate the plight of the poor—or anyone else—until the problems and conditions are properly investigated and analyzed by businesslike methods with successful industry-tested talent.

THE NEED FOR TEETH

The study-and-report procedure is a mill most large corporations have already been through, and many have paid a high price to discover its pitfalls. Social institutions have no unique claim on complex and baffling problems. As an aid to formulating decisions, endless reams of reports are produced on the heels of studies by both internal and external experts.

Nor would any knowledgeable executive deny that scores of wrong reports are being turned out continually by the wrong people for the wrong reasons. But this, I suspect, is the lesser part of the problem. From what I have observed, far more significant is the kind of action or, just as commonly, the inaction, that takes place after the report is produced.

I know of one large consumer products company that three years ago, though it had long since outgrown an unwieldy and inflexible warehouse and distribution network originally set up for a medium-size operation, was still using it. Under this outmoded system, some shipments were lost, others duplicated, others seriously delayed. Inventory control was a shambles. Customer dissatisfaction was eloquent.

Meetings were held by top and middle management. The problems were hashed and rehashed with no agreement reached on what course of action to take. Finally, out of desperation, the company called in a highly regarded outside consultant. After a six-week study he came up with some practical recommendations for revamping and streamlining the system. Specific steps were spelled out, with potential savings documented in each case. At the windup, in an impressive presentation, the consultant and his assistants explained their findings and suggestions, recommended immediate implementation, left a 136-page report with the president, and departed.

More meetings were held. The value of the findings was apparent to all concerned. But political considerations intruded —key jobs would be changed, some posts eliminated. Various balances of power would have to be adjusted. The meetings degenerated into haggling sessions. Executives split up into two main camps, one for reorganization, the other against. The president favored reorganization, but at 62 and close to retirement, was afraid to buck the powerful bloc that was fighting it. Meanwhile the situation reached a crisis, with customers deserting and the market infiltrated by competitors. For the first time in years the traditionally profitable enterprise showed a loss.

At last the board took action. The president was fired and a new man brought in. He studied the reports and the pro and con lineup, fired stubborn executives, put through the change and saved the company in the nick of time.

The point is that no corporation can survive for long if its problems are not effectively analyzed with corrective recommendations reported—and acted upon. It is apparent that social institutions, however, are capable of sponsoring large and expensive studies, reviewing the findings, and reacting with vague promises of "further consideration." After this the neatly bound reports are laid to rest in desk drawers and subsequently transferred to storage archives or warehouses, the ideas contained within left to fade into oblivion.

A report by itself is like a car without a motor. The best report in the world is worthless without the necessary authorization for action.

Our society is filled with talented and experienced businessmen who stand ready to participate in bringing about social change. It abounds with profoundly intelligent and dedicated social planners and administrators. Sophisticated consultants, human engineers, and ecologists are prepared to contribute their knowledge. The new breed of government officials understand the importance of meaningful change and are willing to exert their energies and influence to bring it about. Our research capabilities have been highly developed and refined during the past three decades. We can get the information we need for intelligent decision making and disseminate it efficiently. The problem is not with the technology but with the bureaucracy and the agonizing red tape bureaucracies inevitably engender.

In Sulphur Springs, Texas, a ten-foot-wide strip of parkland was needed for a highway. Local factions recognized the practicality of the use and favored it. But an ordinance required that a report spelling out the impact of highway construction on the environment had to be distributed to and reviewed by 17 different government agencies before approval could be granted. The O.K. finally came through, but it took about two years for this minor move to be made.

On the one hand, society is faced with a critical need for reliable answers to urgent and complex questions, a need that requires intensive research and analysis. On the other hand, bureaucrats, politicians, and a variety of individual axe grinders, for whatever reasons of their own, seize upon "the need for further study and consideration" as a highly effective way to stall decisions and action.

Steven Weisman, a writer for *The New York Times,* provided a vivid picture of what it was like when Mayor John Lindsay took over the reins at New York's city hall:

He was horrified to find that he had no early-warning system to detect potential crises. There was also no formal way for Lindsay to keep tabs on his giant government to see exactly what it was accomplishing. He learned that the work of many departments overlapped, so that one agency might be planning apartments for land already slated for a new road, simply because there was no official information center. There were no statistics on welfare, leaving officials to guess, for instance, how many recipients were actually employable. There was no precise citywide picture of the garbage problem—no one could clearly demonstrate why some streets were dirtier than others. And if the Mayor wanted to learn the current status of a school, a library, or a police precinct nearing construction, his aides had to call public works, or the budget bureau, or the purchase department or the legal department, and ask if they had the papers. "There were no manuals!" a Lindsay aide said recently. "There were no manuals on how things worked!"

With the need for a viable management information system as apparent as it was urgent, the Mayor put internal and external experts to work producing one. Using management science techniques, the experts set up a modern streamlined information-gathering and -analysis network. As the result of creating a planning-programming-budgeting system (PPBS), many reforms and economies were put into effect. Reports were turned out by the hundreds as the aftermath of intensive studies by internal task force analysts and consultants. Many excellent and well-conceived recommendations were made.

Weisman has also provided a graphic description of the difficulties involved in dealing with a bureaucracy:

The experts never told how their proposals were to be carried out. Lindsay tended to believe that once he and his advisers decided on a new way of doing things he could just give the order and it would be done. That tactic worked no better within his own government than it did with the labor unions. Any bureaucracy is a tangle of loyalties to bosses, unions, subordinates, political parties, and individual careers—not just to the man on top. And since Lindsay all along insisted on circumventing the bureaucracy with his new breed of experts, it is not surprising that the city's regular employees—the ones ultimately responsible for carrying out the orders—would respond with less than complete loyalty to their mayor. Lindsay stumbled worst over this problem with his sanitation department, where Budget Bureau analysts measured garbage on the curbs and pored over figures on production and manpower before they proposed changes of garbage truck routes and the use of much bigger trucks. "We had it all figured out," says a former Budget man. "The figures showed the streets would be 85 percent cleaner in six months. Six months passed and there we were, looking at the same filthy streets. Nothing changed except the statistics."

This underlines what is probably the most debilitating shortcoming of our socio-economic system. The great stumbling block to turnaround in our society is not the endless study and investigation that so often seem to stall progress, but the deadly bureaucracy that prevents implementation of recommendations based on findings.

DEVELOPING THE BITE

What we need most in our system are ways to counter bureaucracy when it seeks to settle its prodigious weight upon our attempts at restructuring it. We can provide this resistance in a variety of ways, but it cannot be a byproduct of the system. As SEM prescribes, it must be built right into it.

We can add teeth first of all through the funding and resource-allocation techniques being applied successfully in business today. No company could long survive the fiercely competitive environment of the modern marketplace if it continued paying for programs that did not yield results. Hence the ongoing monitoring of key indicators, which serves to make funds available where objectives are met and to cut them off where they fail. As Arjay Miller, dean of Stanford University Business School and former Ford Motor Company president, points out: "The public sector manager has to take more of a businessman's attitude toward allocating resources."

We have also learned from business that carrots work as well as sticks, and sometimes better. Social reform in the long run is beneficial to all of society. But human beings in general and bureaucrats in particular resist change as a matter of course. Corporate motivation specialists understand this reality of business life and devise a variety of incentives designed to spur individuals to work for innovation instead of against it. We need similar lures in the public sector and new lures as well. We learned with the advent of the computer that our chance for success is considerably enhanced when we *sell* people on change instead of imposing it on them, which only makes them see it as a threat to their security.

Finally, as I have already pointed out, public visibility is a third way of insuring corrective action in response to human needs. We are well into the era of the enlightened consumer. A vast movement is under way to combat inefficiency, corruption, and waste. Consumer advocates, ecologists and conservationists, labor representatives, student and community social responsibility committees, and a growing number of other groups have taken up the cudgels in response to antipublic activities.

Getting back to Socio-Economic Management and the principles of business, one of the most crucial and basic is control. It is in my view the most conspicuously absent in far too many social institutions today. I'm not talking about the routine accounting controls required to insure that transactions are properly recorded, that accounts are in balance, and that attempts at dishonesty are thwarted. What I have in mind is the kind of controls that force action when action is needed, that are implemented as a follow-through to monitoring and measurement. When we have such controls in force—and this is an important part of the thrust of Socio-Economic Management—we provide maximum assurance that organizational goals will be reached, whether they relate to corporate profits or to human needs.

4

TARGETS
FOR SURVIVAL

One of the hindrances to social reform in our time is that we grow weary of the tired old precepts that are hammered at us year after year after year. The one having to do with the "setting of goals" and "ordering of priorities" is a prime example. How often has the critical importance of realistic, well targeted, clearly stated objectives been driven home to us in recent years? So often, I fear, that when we hear the admonition today we heed it with half an ear or less. Or worse, we wince and dismiss it as another platitude.

So what should we do? Discontinue our emphasis on goals in favor of some new and fresh precept? Unfortunately we cannot afford this luxury. When we stop focusing on goals, we stop focusing on progress. Platitude or not, the hard fact remains that no business enterprise could survive for long were not profit goals set, monitored, and measured with at least a reasonable degree of efficiency. Platitude or not, and no matter how basic, simple, and obvious the goal-setting principle may be, the effective establishment of objectives is what results and performance are all about.

A goal is a milestone against which actions and results can be compared with expectations and commitments. It is the basis for evaluating program effectiveness and merit. Only by means of forward-looking goals are we able to formulate plans that aim at qualitative accomplishments instead of numbers. As experience has proved on innumerable occasions, the clearer and more meaningful the goals, the more effective and responsive to needs the organization.

Goals trigger action. When a well-run business defines as a profit objective new market penetration, it budgets for newspaper and television advertising, direct mail solicitations, introductory product discounts, and other promotions. When it measures results, it does not merely tally the pieces—number of advertising lines, number of TV commercials, number of promotional mailings, number of discounted items sold. Rather it asks: For these inputs, these expenditures, how much of the market did we penetrate and how profitable is the penetration? How much in the way of repeat sales and profits can we expect? The goal is clearly spelled out, and the manager who dismissed it as a platitude would himself be dismissed as incompetent.

By contrast, how many social agencies assess their actions in terms of *social* profitability by asking: To what extent did we fulfill client needs? How much "repeat business"—continued needs fulfillment—can we expect? Surprisingly few. The reality is that most social organizations pursue the kind of nontargeted course that, followed by a commercial enterprise, would mean almost certain failure.

EFFICIENCY IS CRUCIAL

The tragic consequence of nontargeted social activity is an intolerable squandering of public resources already in distressingly short supply. Between now and 1976, a Brookings Institution report makes clear, existing federal programs will use up nearly all of the extra federal revenue generated by the growth of the national economy, the so-called fiscal dividend.

Quite simply, what this means is that in most cases ambitious new programs will be financed by new taxation, cuts in existing programs, or not at all. Otherwise, *Wall Street Journal* writer George Melloan is convinced that there will be deficits that would exceed hypothetical full-employment revenues, and those would be very serious deficits for the economy. He feels that the thing to keep in mind is that the mortgage on the future is already heavy. So much so that increasingly choices will not be between two desirables we don't have but between a desirable we don't have and giving up one we do have. That, of course, is a considerably harder choice.

Are today's social goals being formulated with this kind of urgency in mind? Here and there, perhaps. But the great mass of public programs are little more than a habitual perpetuation of the numbers game. Welfare programs continue to tally the number of mouths to be fed, poverty housing units built, dollars doled out.

But what is our real objective in welfare? Isn't it to make people employable, self-sufficient, productive, and happy by helping them achieve self-respect? Those responsible for the purse strings rarely apply this kind of standard to our outputs. Yet the proper criteria for evaluating the effectiveness of welfare programs are renewed human beings, not numbers on a sheet. And the techniques for such measurement are available.

Our prison programs are equally piece-oriented: number of prison cells maintained, number of prisoners housed. It is on the basis of these figures that money is allocated. What prison officials should be measuring, however, is the number of men and women they rehabilitate in return for the money granted them. They should be evaluating prison programs and facilities on the basis of contributions made to rehabilitation. And they should be projecting the degree of rehabilitation that will result from this year's investment. After all, this is what "corrective" incarceration is supposed to be about.

Former Attorney General Ramsey Clark tells us that virtually the entire prison population suffers from either alcoholism, narcotics addiction, or mental instability. Shouldn't this steer us to the kind of goals we should be setting and the programs to which our resources should be allocated? Instead of earmarking massive sums for stronger cell blocks and tougher guards, might we not benefit from facilities and activities designed to help cure the prisoners? Shouldn't the main thrust of our effort be made in areas of tested and proven needs fulfillment as determined by our monitoring and measurement processes? As they are presently constituted, our penal institutions are geared more toward the hardening of criminals and the multiplication of recidivism than the rehabilitation of troubled men and women.

NEEDS, NOT NUMBERS

It is a simple axiom of good business management that when the executive team loses sight of profit objectives, critical problems arise. The identical situation occurs when social managers perpetuate untargeted activities, or when they gear programs to goals that are unrelated to the fulfillment of client needs.

As always, the starting point is needs. When needs are improperly identified, bypassed, or ignored, social programs wind up in the red.

In the study of health services in the city of Newark prepared by The Center for Analysis of Public Issues, one finding is typical not only of Newark but of funding in communities across the nation. The city and the board of education were asked by the study group to discontinue two dental clinics costing the community $300,000 a year. Public and parochial school examinations, it was noted, had ceased two years before. Though tests were never resumed, the funding continued. What the operation consisted of at the time of the report was 31 part-time dentists working short hours who, more often than not, failed to show up. Transferring dental care to five neighborhood centers, four already in existence and one on the way, would be one way to respond to client needs far more effectively and economically.

I am frequently asked by concerned citizens: "How can Socio-Economic Management be translated from theory into practice?"

The simplest answer of all lies in asking the right questions. In this dental care situation, for example, were those publicly funded facilities properly goal-directed in their operation during the past two years? Were they fulfilling human needs as efficiently as possible? Had these questions been honestly posed and objectively replied to six, twelve, or eighteen months ago, would the clinics still be in operation two years after their usefulness had been outlived?

If, starting tomorrow, each administrator, each official, each budget manager were to ask: "Is this operation responding to human needs in the best possible way?" just think to what degree the effectiveness of our social programs might be multiplied.

Granted, there are some who, for a variety of reasons, prefer not to ask this question. Yet it has been my experience that for every selfish bureaucrat there are several dedicated ones. Still it would be a great mistake to disregard the weaknesses of human nature. Some administrators would go to any extreme to avoid relinquishing their fiefdoms. Others are so entrenched in bureaucracy they are unable to see the goals through the numbers. The social sector, of course, boasts no monopoly when it comes to bureaucracy. It exists throughout our society, in our major corporations as well as in our social institutions. The trouble is that the institutions have the greater tolerance for inefficiency and waste. If a corporation is clogged by bureaucracy beyond a certain point, it will founder. Institutional inertia simply produces the continued erosion of public resources and deferment of needs fulfillment.

Through it all the agencies persist and even flourish in terms of appropriations and size as the population they are failing to serve continues to grow. This nagging problem is of great concern to a host of conscientious social planners and government officials who fear that time, along with the wellsprings of funding, is running out.

Senator Jack Miller of Iowa believes that the human element is playing less and less a role in the big business of government. He maintains that the face-to-face relationship is being replaced by systems of communications, transaction forms, reports, instructions, and other record-making and record-using techniques; by employers whose labors consist for the most part in processing paperwork at a cost of around $10 billion annually.

Senator Warren Magnuson echoes this view. Congress, he points out, is still attempting, quite literally, "to run a business ten times as large as AT&T and General Motors combined with machinery as obsolete as a quill pen and a slanting bookkeeper's desk."

The implicit plea of both of these men is for a nationwide system of Socio-Economic Management, a system that starts with human needs and is built on specific, time-committed, monitorable, and measurable goals designed to satisfy them.

What is wrong with many of the goals we have today? Senator Miller poses three factors that at least partly explain the planning inadequacy:

1. In the selection of a problem, Congress too frequently moves on the basis of what is headline-making or eye-catching, rather than on what will be critical in the years ahead. It selects problems that promise almost immediate political results. Problems that do not offer immediate payback opportunities are usually deferred until they reach crisis proportions and no longer can be ignored.

2. In defining the problem, Congress too frequently is satisfied with ambiguities, so that implementation of what is enacted is too broad in scope to avoid confusion; or it oversimplifies, so that only one aspect of the problem is considered—thus leaving important gaps in its ultimate solution.

3. In stating the objectives and establishing criteria by which results will be judged, Congress too frequently fails to question the advisability and feasibility of a program, and just goes ahead and spends money on it anyhow.

The most glaring lack is the lack of controls, modern business-type controls. With proper controls, as advocated under Socio-Economic Management, individual ambitions and foibles cannot take precedence over objectives designed to achieve productivity and profitability, whether business or social. When a well-run corporation strays off target, key business indicators are automatically tripped to alert management. Sales fall. Inventories pile up. Labor rates increase. Lead times stretch. Material yield alters. Immediately a red flag waves. Management snaps into action to make the adjustments required to get the vessel back on course. Either that, or it revises the assumptions upon which targets are based.

In an era when change is as constant as Old Faithful, the prospect of running a company without continuous monitoring, measurement, and adjustment would make a seasoned chief executive blanch. Yet these basic ingredients of sound modern management are conspicuously missing from a majority of U.S. agencies and nonprofit institutions.

We can no longer afford to run the massive organizations of the seventies with the tools of the forties. When the excavation is huge we must lay aside our picks and shovels and apply the giant earthmoving equipment on hand. Key social indicators, for example, can be established and monitored every bit as effectively as key business indicators. We can use employment fluctuations, incidence of violence and unrest, amount of pollution in water or air, frequency of client complaints, amount of illness or crime, evidence of community pride, and upgraded levels of reading and other skills to guide us in evaluating social programs, testing our goals, and measuring progress.

So-called early warning systems that go under a variety of labels have been installed and are working successfully in scores of corporations. The establishment of modern management controls has been honed down to a matter of routine. The technology exists. It has been tested and proved in both public and private organizations. And the expertise is available to make the technology work.

To outline the "how to" of controls implementation would take a book in itself. And what purpose would it serve? The "how to" has been documented in scores of textbooks. It is on file in the offices of management consultants, in accounting firms, in the systems departments of large corporations and in the sprinkling of nonprofit institutions and agencies where they already have been installed. Only one thing remains to be done: to apply the know-how on a wide-ranging national basis regardless of how many boats are rocked in the process. There lies the bottleneck.

ANTICIPATE RESULTS

The anticipation and spelling out of end results can be a powerful weapon in the structuring of social goals and strategies. As Leo A. Molinaro, president of American City Corporation, puts it, "I know of at least a hundred cities that have had studies made of trends in their local economy and other basic life-support systems. Perhaps another hundred cities can be found that have attempted to establish goals. But I have yet to find a city that tries to spell out in clear, operational terms just what life could be like if the city could achieve its objectives and reverse undesirable trends or reinforce desirable ones."

Molinaro goes on to explain that the consequence of our goals must be anticipated. We must spell out in advance what their achievement will mean in terms of how we live, play, work, rest, communicate, raise our families, worship, organize, politic, and dissent. "The questions of relevance and honesty," he concludes, "raised so painfully by our high school and college students, deal precisely with this point. They want to know not only where they are going but what difference it will make if they get there." What he is saying, in brief, is that there must be a visible benefit for every cost and a visible return on every investment if the new environment is to be maintained by those who live in it.

When you boil it down, what is an objective if not the end state of a condition after action has been taken? Describing this end state in clear and specific terms and setting a time for its achievement is the essence of goal setting and the criterion for progress reporting. When we fail in our social programs to anticipate end results and keep our sights fixed on their fulfillment we start wandering in diverse directions. Objectives are broadly and vaguely defined, the possibility of waste and inefficiency multiplied.

Appalachia is a prime example. During the sixties more than $2 billion in federal funds were poured into those 13 blighted states. The objective presumably was to alleviate the plight of the poor.

If this was the goal, it is apparent by now that a variety of end results were formulated in a number of different minds regarding precisely what the massive funding was supposed to accomplish.

As a *New York Times* editorial states,

The infusion of federal money into Appalachia has helped redistribute wealth to one of the poorer sections of the country, but it has not reached the really poor who need help. Of $1.1 billion originally authorized, $840 million—more than three-quarters of the total—was earmarked for highways. Most of the rest of the money was allocated for construction projects such as regional health centers, vocational schools, and airports. As one commission official has said, "It's a brick-and-mortar program rather than a people program."

As a result, the Appalachian regional program mostly helps those who are already well up the economic ladder—merchants, bankers, coal mine owners, industrialists, road builders. The fringes of the region which has always been better off have also shown economic progress. But the persons who live in what most people think of as Appalachia—the rural poor in West Virginia and eastern Kentucky—have scarcely been touched by all this federal spending.

In setting goals, the importance of identifying the end state desired and gearing actions and measurement accordingly is obvious. In the case of Appalachia the questions virtually pose themselves. Was the overriding purpose of the federal funding to improve transportation and thus bring more business to merchants and help businessmen to move goods more efficiently? If not, why was the bulk of the money spent on highways and airports? Obviously, better roads promote employment in industrial centers already established. But was the program designed to reach the most desperately poor in outlying districts where help was most critically needed? Apparently not.

Similar considerations are applicable in other fields of social service. How many billions, for example, did we pour into expenditures designed to improve health-care delivery during the past decade? And how many more billions have already been allocated for the years ahead? Since there has been no significant increase in male longevity over the past ten years, isn't it just possible we are failing to project what the end state will be as a result of the funding? And aren't we also found lacking in trying to achieve the goals we set up?

The answer to this question emerges in the diversity of proposed solutions touted within the medical community itself. One expert claims the primary answer to health care lies in improved hospital productivity. Another advocates drastic action to reduce the so-called "doctor shortage" as quickly as possible. A third fervently urges the accelerated training of, not physicians, but physician's aides and other paramedical personnel to free up doctors' time. Still another thinks that the real solution lies in education—not education of medical students, however, but of the health care recipients themselves. If dietary habits could be changed, his argument goes, weight brought down, regular exercise programs adhered to, and cigarette smoking stopped, the need for health service would be drastically reduced.

Which advocate is right? All of them, probably. But in which direction should we proceed? What goals should be set and how should they be ranked in importance? What financial and human resources should be allocated to each?

The weighing of alternatives is infinitely complex. It is complex in business, too, and companies cannot be too far off in their decision making and survive—as is not the case with social institutions. In a corporation too, a similar set of questions might be posed in attempting, through the establishment of effective subobjectives, to fulfill the overriding goal of increased profitability. Should investment money be set aside for acquisitions? To develop new products? To increase manpower training? To seek new markets and distribution channels?

The successful large corporation takes all of these steps and allocates resources in proportion to the expectations for each alternative. Though the decisions are never infallible, the guesswork is reduced to a minimum by means of research, analysis, and computerized techniques. And these are as available to the social planner as they are to the business executive.

VALUE INCENTIVES

Here is a simple illustration of how value standards based on met human needs might be implemented by the federal government. Let us take three hypothetical communities: New City, Modern City, and Old City. New City, with a population of 95,000, received a federal grant of $10 million last year for its poverty programs. Modern City, with the same population and economic status, received $9 million. Old City, a carbon copy of the other two, received only $8 million.

Why the disparity?

The criterion is end results. In the last fiscal year, New City, through effective programs imaginatively administered, succeeded in making 1,000 indigent clients employable and self-sufficient; Modern City returned 500 citizens to the economic mainstream; Old City only 50. The federal government, relating appropriations to end results first identified, then achieved, applied a value standard to a poverty effort. Basically, this is the kind of action Socio-Economic Management is set up to perform.

It would work similarly for other social institutions focusing on end results and setting standards accordingly. Under a penal program, for example, Prison A, having rehabilitated 100 prisoners last year, would receive an appropriation of $200,000 above its minimal needs for the coming year. Prison B, with 50 prisoners made into productive citizens, would receive an extra $100,000. Prison C, with no rehabilitations, would get nothing. In fact, thoughtful probing would take place to determine what Prison C is doing wrong that the other institutions are doing right. It would then have to either alter its programs or be placed under new management.

Penal administration under this system would provide an extra $2,000 for each released prisoner rehabilitated during the year. The additional funds, used at the discretion of the prison administrator, would make available for successful and imaginative managers the means to do more of the same. Qualitative standards, in short, would play a key role in the allocation of resources by the officials in charge of funding.

Incentives and disincentives of this kind are familiar tools to profit-minded businessmen. In New York City, a controversial study by the city administrator's staff revealed that sanitation department collection costs are $49 a ton. Private carting companies, which serve restaurants, hotels, and many other private businesses, do the same job for $17.50 a ton, a little more than a third of the public cost. The difference is disquieting to the officials concerned.

Since 1968 the city has bought more than 1,200 new trucks in the hope that doing so would boost productivity by 20 percent over the old models. It didn't work that way. In fact, no improvement at all was registered. Does it not seem reasonable that qualitative standards used so effectively to run a modern business profitably might have some bearing at least on this performance disparity?

NEEDED: A DATA BASE FOR VALID GOALS

How many people do you know today who are against clean air and water? Against scenic beauty? Effective crime control? Eliminating poverty? Providing decent housing and employment for all Americans? Delivering high quality health care to our nation's poor and disadvantaged?

There is a basic human decency in all of us. When a close relative becomes seriously ill, one spares no expense in restoring him to health. It is the same with social programs designed to improve the human condition. The notion that a prosperous society might not be able to afford the financial cost of cleaning up the environment, for example, would trigger the indignation of many U.S. citizens, particularly in light of the billions being spent on "defense." The concept of investment in social renewal, in short, has become as acceptable and popular as freedom of religion or the press.

It is a healthful and constructive attitude, to be sure. But it is not without its pitfalls, for, under the pressures of a greatly accelerated social awakening, our nation is undertaking unprecedented programs without adequate knowledge of the costs involved.

It is one thing to resolve to make the investment that has to be made for social restructuring to take place. It is quite another to continue pouring vast amounts of our shrinking capital into social endeavors when there is no evidence that the condition deplored will be ameliorated.

In Watts, for example, as we shall see toward the end of this book, almost a quarter of a billion dollars has been spent, presumably to bring new hope and light to a desperate community. What the noble crusade deteriorated into, however, was a gigantic spending spree with half the funds going for administration and paperwork and more millions toted out of Watts by professional do-gooders who did well for themselves alone. As a result, the tragic reality is that Watts today is no better off in terms of jobs and living conditions than it was in 1965 when the riots occurred.

Again it might be well to bring the corporate parallel to mind. Crises erupt in business as they do in society. XYZ Corporation, let us say, has been rapidly losing its market share because of innovations made by a leading competitor. Should it fold up that part of the business? Engage in an all-out product development effort? Expand and restructure the marketing organization? Clearly, a major investment will be required if the company is to survive. Suggestions and proposals start pouring into the chief executive from experts and managers inside and out. How does he respond? By exclaiming enthusiastically "That's a great idea, Bill, let's try it"? Or, "Good thinking, Al, we'll give it a whirl"? Or, "We'll put a million dollars into this and see how it works"? Not at all. Not in business.

In business, proposals involving major expenditures are processed through tough and critical evaluation mills. A variety of modern financial tools and techniques are applied, some of which are briefly discussed in this book. Costs are carefully analyzed and tradeoffs considered. What emerges is no infallible decision or plan, but the *best* decision and plan that is obtainable after the same business management principles now embodied in SEM precepts are applied. And they emerge with a better chance of accomplishing valid objectives.

The burning question is this. Are our social programs less pressing and critical than our business programs? Can we afford to disregard in our social institutions the techniques we have developed in business to produce at least a reasonable degree of efficiency? How many more Wattses, Newarks, and Detroits can we sustain?

Out of a federal budget exceeding $200 billion, how much should we spend on poverty? The question is both mind-boggling and complex. Is it conceivable that viable answers could come out of numbers-based guesswork? What about space? How much should we invest? In missiles? Submarines? Aircraft? The military establishment in general?

Are we spending enough money on education? Too much on transportation? To what extent should public funds support the skyrocketing costs of health care? Is $2¼ billion too much or too little to spend on emergency employment programs designed to create federal, state, and municipal jobs?

Some of these questions may be all but unanswerable. But we are going to have to cope with them whether we like it or not. And in formulating some of the answers, we cannot brush aside political considerations. However, one thing is certain. Before valid goals can be developed and end states defined, we must understand the comparative costs to society of the main alternatives involved.

Hans S. Landsberg of Resources for the Future, Inc., cites a typical example to underline the importance of cost-benefit analysis in determining goals. "If the effluent from a paper mill muddies the water for the downstream resident, and the cost of removing the cause exceeds the cost of reducing such disturbance by treatment at the intake, it would clearly be efficient to let the offending effluent continue and to treat the water prior to its further use."

Here is the base from which we start. With this in mind practical decisions can be made. The "winner," or paper mill, Landsberg continues, could compensate the "loser," or municipality, out of savings that would accrue from not having to treat the effluent. Thus both efficiency and equity would be served.

"When we can compare meaningfully the costs to society," the resources specialist concludes, "with the many-sided benefits that are the counterpart of those costs, we shall have taken a long stride toward evolving a workable policy of preserving the quality of the environment without sacrificing the beneficial effects of advancing technology."

Again, to labor a familiar SEM theme, the techniques of comparison are available and documented to the hilt.

OBJECTIVES BEGIN IN THE MARKETPLACE

It would be rare to find any organization, private or public, that thinks through its objectives infallibly. In principle, social objectives are no different from business objectives. Both are based on assumptions made at the time of their formulation. Assumptions are based on conditions evaluated as a result of "market" intelligence. Conditions, which are always changing, are based on the requirements and desires of people.

In the modern corporation, getting an accurate fix on customer needs is of overriding importance to the marketing organization. Programs are constantly being devised to test rapidly changing needs and moods and preferences. However sophisticated the techniques applied and the computer programs designed to digest and process this information, what it boils down to in the end is a two-way exchange between supplier and supplied. The marketer asks in effect, "What business *should* we be in?" And if the research job has been done properly, the customer tells him.

The social planner is no less intelligent than the business planner and no less sensitive to the impact of change. But again, the pressures of the social institution to respond to real client needs are not nearly so urgent from the standpoint of organizational survival. The musical-instrument manufacturer who peddles cellos in a rock-band market would not survive for long. And the fellow in charge of the selling effort had better know it.

Not so the social manager. His job is at least temporarily secure whether he responds effectively to client needs or not. Institutional survival simply is not geared to market acceptance, as it is in the commercial sector.

Hence in prisons we witness Archie Bunker-type programs designed for the mentally disturbed. We see educational institutions stubbornly clinging to rigidly time-slotted classroom traditions established generations ago when the United States had a farm economy. We see massive welfare giveaways that create more hostility than gratitude. Nor do they begin to meet real human needs or develop self-sufficiency and self-respect.

Yet the programs persist because, no matter how poor the institutional performance, institutional shutdown is rarely threatened. As we grope more and more desperately for solutions to our complex social problems, the illusion is perpetuated that the answer lies in the numbers—as if more prisons, more schools, more welfare programs, more policemen, more doctors, more training centers will somehow provide a panacea.

We are kidding ourselves. A hillside of evidence has demonstrated that whatever the ultimate solution to our social ills may be, one thing is certain: From an institutional standpoint, it is not more of the same.

The harsh reality of social administration is that in too many instances, the institutions have lost touch with the individuals they have been created to serve.

In the public sector, institutional wheels are turned by tax-payer dollars and citizen votes. Thus, institutional "shareholders and consumers," or the public, must rightly exercise a measure of control. The nonprofit institution can be justified by one criterion only: its measure of effectiveness in responding to the needs of its clients. If these needs are to be properly identified, clarified, ranked in order of priority, and translated into attainable organizational goals, the public must be consulted.

It is an overridingly important function of Socio-Economic Management to make sure that this occurs.

5

THE
MANAGEMENT
OF SURVIVAL

On May 8, 1971, columnist Jack Anderson reported on the establishment of the American Revolution Bicentennial Commission, located across the street from the White House. Its sole purpose is to plan an appropriate celebration of the 200th anniversary.

Headed by a $25,000-a-year Navy captain, according to Anderson, the commission "is populated with high-paid, highfalutin' bureaucrats who work in magnificent surroundings with chauffeur-driven cars furnished by the Pentagon to whisk them around Washington on their mysterious missions."

Staff members, his report continues, possess the special skill absolutely essential to bureaucratic success: "the talent for complication, for making simplicities complex, sociology textbooks out of common sense." The meetings, we are told, are planned in the same fastidious detail that a Big Four summit conference might receive. Preparations are so elaborate a special booklet has been printed to enumerate them. This document devotes considerable space to coffee breaks, which, Anderson wryly asserts, seem to be more frequent than any other activity. The precise number of ashtrays, ice water pitchers, drinking glasses, and wastebaskets are specified for each meeting room.

Without underrating the importance of our 200th anniversary celebration, we must concede that it surely would rank below such needs as poverty, health care, crime, and narcotics control on our list of national priorities. Something is clearly wrong with a management system that would permit such questionable application of our financial resources.

Nor is this commission an isolated example. Countless cases could be cited to point up administrative inadequacies in publicly funded programs covering virtually all fields of social activity.

Education will serve as well as any. For a specific illustration we need look no further than the comprehensive evaluation of instructional technology made recently by the Academy for Educational Development. The study disclosed that millions of dollars worth of learning machines, language laboratories, film, TV, and other audiovisual equipment were either gathering dust or being sadly underutilized. The technology's exciting potential is undeniable. But much of it is too complicated for undertrained teachers to use. Nor is the system sufficiently flexible to adjust to the change that would be required if the potential were to be realized.

At higher levels of education, as Leo L. Kornfeld, director of education services for the management consulting firm of Cresap, McCormick and Paget, points out, many universities are more complex and have bigger budgets than the largest corporations. They are also, in many respects, more difficult to manage.

When the war nobody wants finally comes to an end, we shall still have unrest on college campuses unless glaring inadequacies in university administration are faced realistically and effective solutions found. New management concepts are urgently needed to meet problems of bigness, administrative complexity . . . and rising educational standards, student expectations, and social demands —all within the framework of relentlessly increasing costs.

From all sectors the cry for more effective management is heard—for a system that spells out goals, pinpoints executive responsibility, and provides the needed authority to meet objectives. The alternative is decision paralysis.

A case in point was Westinghouse Electric Corporation's proposed transit expressway for the city of Pittsburgh some years ago. In response to an urgent presidential appeal for upgraded low-cost urban transportation, the designers came up with a plan that called for overhead construction alongside automobile lanes. As designed, notes George Cabot Lodge, an associate professor of Business Administration at Harvard, the expressway offered fast, frequent, safe, and comfortable service at minimum cost.

Three government agencies, one federal and two state, joined Westinghouse in funding that exceeded $5 million for a test and demonstration. The results were successful, the system was found to be sufficiently flexible to meet the transit needs of medium-size cities. Visiting mayors and transit authorities were enthusiastic. Yet the program bogged down.

Despite their enthusiasm, officials lacked the authority and influence to get the plan approved. The ultimate decision makers, consultants to the authorities, opposed it simply because of the risk of an innovative system. The problem was compounded by formidable bidding and funding procedures. Added to this were the powerful highway and gasoline lobbies. Understandably, the gears became so enmeshed in red tape that the machinery ground to a halt. There was not one manager with the authority to say, "For Pete's sake, it works. Let's do it!"

Sold on the concept's value, Westinghouse persevered and has since installed systems in airports and amusement parks—while the problems of urban transit grow progressively worse.

The task, as Lodge concludes, "requires the renovation of the authority and strength of government at all levels. . . . Business can play an important role; but it will only delay the process and tempt disaster if it seeks to take on the task itself before the way is clear." Made clear, we might add, by a viable system of Socio-Economic Management.

America, long the world's acknowledged leader and pioneer in the creation and implementation of advanced management techniques, certainly possesses the capability to produce such a system. Yet in recent years and in expanding areas of social involvement, other nations have been showing us how the job should be done. The Japanese, for example, have shown that by adapting U.S. management expertise to their own social and business complex they can, in many areas, outperform the West.

THE ACHIEVABLE POTENTIAL

The prospects are not totally bleak. A growing awareness has developed in widening segments of our society of the need for upgraded management of our nonprofit institutions and programs. An informal survey of small-college presidents indicates they are spending from 40 to 60 percent of their time on business and management duties, up sharply from previous years. Harvard, Stanford, Tulane, and other universities are engaged in programs that apply proven business techniques to college operations. Senator Mondale and other legislators long have been hammering home the urgency of improved social management in congressional hearings.

The Academy for Educational Development, Inc. has established a management division under grants from the W. K. Kellogg Foundation with Olin Corporation and others participating as donors. This group conducts research on urgent management problems, and communicates its findings through seminars, mailings, and a planned information center. Its purpose, as stated by Eurich, is "to help that college president who, when he can't stand the heat in the kitchen, is tempted to put his head in the oven."

So a start has been made, and at times it is heartening. But it is also on a small scale. It is all the more frustrating when one thinks of what could be accomplished starting today.

"If we can get to the moon. . . ."

The phrase has become a cliché. But cliché or not, landing a man on the moon is regarded by many to have been the most complex task ever undertaken by man. At the program's peak, some 20,000 companies employing millions of people supplied equipment, material, and services for Apollo. Many of the firms were fiercely competitive. They worked with government agencies, with universities, with each other under the tightest of schedules and most rigid conditions. They were pressured and monitored to the hilt. Some of the technical and logistical problems were almost frightening to contemplate—not to mention the problems of human endurance. The command module alone contained two million functional parts, excluding wires and skeletal components.

Yet the goal was achieved without unreasonably exceeding the budget projected, and well ahead of schedule. It was achieved because the goals, the plans, the schedules, the organization, the measurement, the incentives—all the ingredients of Socio-Economic Management—were included in the program.

In a *Fortune* article, writer Tom Alexander asks *that* question: "If we can send men to the moon, why can't we eradicate pollution, or cure poverty, or rebuild cities?"

We can.

Perhaps, in reflecting on such achievements as Apollo, we have been concentrating too hard on the project's technical accomplishment. As Alexander points out: "The really significant fallout from the strains, traumas, and endless experimentation of Project Apollo has been of a sociological rather than a technological nature: techniques for directing the massed endeavors of scores of thousands of minds in a close-knit, mutually enhancive combination of government, university, and private industry."

He is referring to management.

THE DANGEROUS GAME OF "SURPRISE!"

In the hearings of the Special Subcommittee on Evaluation and Planning of Social Programs of which he is chairman, Senator Mondale asked Washington attorney Joseph A. Califano, Jr.:

You were in the White House, I believe, when the cities started exploding with racial tensions, Newark and the rest, in 1967. Were those eruptions anticipated? When they occurred, was there readily available to the President any information to quickly explain what happened and why, what caused them? Was there that kind of social data?

No, Mr. Chairman, there wasn't.

Would you say that took the country by surprise?

I think it did. I think Watts, which was in the summer of 1965, took the country by surprise. Even there, if you just take that small area, there was no social data available on it . . . .

The point is that whether you're running a social enterprise or a business enterprise, surprise can be costly and devastating.

But surprise can be minimized. Under a well-structured management information system, it can be substantially reduced. This has been demonstrated in scores of U.S. corporations. In Varian Associates Aerograph Division, for example, a program called TRACC is in force. An acronym for target review and adjustment for continuous control, TRACC is primarily an early warning system. Its function is to minimize the kind of surprise that defeats profit objectives in the company's operation.

At the program's core is a series of key indicators—labor rates, price, material yield, order lead time, and many others. The indicators are used in part to test assumptions on which important decisions have been made. The reasoning is that assumptions rarely remain static. Because of changing conditions —which change at least as fast in social programs—what applies today may not apply tomorrow.

Serious problems develop when vital assumptions suddenly become invalid. TRACC's function is to create an awareness of this as early as possible so that adjustment can be made before serious loss is incurred. Under the system, management is automatically alerted when variance limitations established by the key indicators are exceeded.

Several such advanced management information systems are in operation today. TRACC is just one of them. The concept is well past the testing stage. It has been applied repeatedly, and it works.

There is an abundance of computer systems, but why are they only rarely, if ever, effectively applied to complex social programs, where the need is the greatest? One reason is that before a management information system geared to cope with change can be made to work, the management structure itself must be made goal-oriented, results-oriented, and viable.

The more accelerated the rate of change in a society, the more vulnerable are its business and social institutions to surprise. As Toffler tells us in *Future Shock,*

In the three short decades between now and the twenty-first century, millions of ordinary, psychologically normal people will face an abrupt collision with the future. Citizens of the world's richest and most technologically advanced nations, many of them will find it increasingly painful to keep up with the incessant demand for change that characterizes our time. For them, the future will have arrived too soon.

The anxiety generated by this head-on collision is sharply intensified by expanding diversity. Incontrovertible evidence shows that increasing the number of choices to an individual also increases the amount of information he needs to process if he is to deal with them. Laboratory tests on men and animals alike prove that the more choices, the slower the reaction time. It is the frontal collision of these three incompatible demands that is now producing a decision-making crisis in the techno-societies.

And, it might be added, helping to produce confusion and immobility in some of our social institutions.

According to Darwinian theory, the species most capable of adapting to dynamically changing conditions is the one with the best survival potential. In today's change-jolted society we could expand this to include social and business organizations as well. What's more, evidence increasingly links the potential for survival to the ability to change.

It also follows that the more demanding the change, the more structured and streamlined the system for dealing with it must be. Over the long haul this could well be the most compelling reason of all to apply the proven management techniques of business more extensively to our complex social programs.

ZERO IN ON RESULTS

The professionally managed business organization does not take results for granted. Nor does it take individual or departmental performance for granted. Established and accepted business management practice is by no means confined to advanced and exotic techniques.

In remarks addressed to the Committee for Economic Development, Marvin Bower, managing director of McKinsey & Co., stated:

Industry experience also shows that rigorous evaluations are most effective when backed with knowledge that poor performance can result in job transfers or separations. Government regulations and practices now make such results so unlikely that productivity is more difficult of achievement. Such a negative incentive—even though sparingly used—is an essential ingredient for full productivity in any kind of group effort.

Automatically assumed in managing a business, the power to fire an employee is woefully lacking in government agencies and other nonprofit organizations. Under the existing bureaucracy, discharging a subordinate for misconduct or unsatisfactory performance, while possible, is usually so complicated and costly in terms of time and energy that few officials have the temerity to challenge the system. Similarly, compensation incentives and disincentives are ineffectively administered. Consider the Salary Reform Act of 1962. Under it, authority was granted to deny within-grade pay raises for Civil Service Commission employees who perform below an acceptable level of competence and to allow within-grade increases for those with outstanding records. Reports indicate that only an infinitesimal percentage of agency personnel were affected by this added discretion. Thus, even where beneficial high management decisions are made, the structure's creaky intermediate management system is inadequate for proper implementation.

A PERPLEXING CHOICE

Like the products we use, each social commodity ingested by our system comes at a cost, at times direct and apparent, at times frustratingly circuitous. Sometimes the cost is deferred by bond issues and other means, or transferred from one sector of society to another. Virtually always, the costs—and the benefits, which presumably derive from the costs—interact to a perplexing degree.

Social managers and administrators are confronted by no problem more frustrating than that of choosing which resources to allocate for which program where. How much of our nation's money and manpower should we devote to purify the air and waterways, control narcotics, upgrade the level of health care, curb crime, provide better education, housing, transportation, recreation? Even if this question could be simply resolved, how does one determine which programs, which institutions, and which subagencies are most effective in responding to and reducing human needs? Where, in short, will our input produce the best output?

If we could answer this question to perfection, we might create a perfect society. Needless to say, perfection doesn't exist and couldn't. But that doesn't mean we shouldn't shoot for perfection and score, if not a bull's-eye, at least a respectable hit. There are proven management techniques to insure that program alternatives are selected rationally and scientifically after intelligent evaluation of the major factors and evidence on hand. This is a giant stride from the eeny-meeny-miney-mo guesswork politico-numbers how-we-always-did-it methodology so often in force today.

One such technique, thoroughly tested and widely applied in business management, is cost-benefit analysis. Another is the related, more broadly structured concept of PPBS, or planning-programming-budgeting system. Both these approaches of systems analysis techniques were applied by the Defense Department in the days of Secretary Robert S. McNamara. Some are being applied to social programs today, but primarily on a quantitative basis. Evidence exists to show that the technical and managerial capabilities are on hand to apply them qualitatively as well.

Only when we can meaningfully compare our human and financial inputs against value of outputs produced will we properly be able to evaluate the mushrooming buildup of program alternatives in our society—a monumental task, to be sure. But we proved we can do it. We did it in Apollo. We're doing it in business.

Some will argue, of course, that society's problems are different and infinitely more complex than those facing business. Maybe so—but complex problems can be broken down to manageable dimensions. Granting the complexity of our social behemoth, what better argument could we want to underline the need for a more systematic methodology for selecting the proper alternatives? As evidence affirms repeatedly, the more complex the problem, the more pressing the need for a scientifically structured approach.

Cost-benefit analysis, qualitatively and quantitatively applied, provides just that. It breaks programs down to their basic cost and value elements. This becomes the basis for assessment, with value of output per dollar compared for program alternatives.

The Conference Board points out: "Each benefit-cost ratio indicates by how many times total (capitalized) dollar benefits exceed total (capitalized) dollar costs. Cost-effectiveness analysis thus permits the ranking of alternative government programs according to the degree of economic efficiency with which they achieve their goal."

Today we can measure social efficiency as well, but such strategies could not be made to work in an archaic managerial environment. To illustrate the concept's potential, the Conference Board uses a 1966 HEW study of government programs designed to reduce injuries and deaths from traffic accidents.

"There are very large variations in the dollar savings," the report continues, "from reduced traffic injuries and deaths per dollar of program costs. (These savings measure the reductions in medical expenses and in lost income due to traffic injuries, and the capitalized future lifetime earnings in the case of deaths.) By far the largest savings per dollar of program cost (well over $1,000) are associated with two of the three least expensive programs; by far the smallest savings (less than $3), with the two most expensive programs."

The management alternatives are clear: proven strategies such as cost-benefit analysis for evaluating programs even if we reduce all elements to quantifiable dollars and cents, or the kind of mindless reasoning that goes, "Well, let's see now, how much did we appropriate last year?" Or, how many diplomas were handed out, crimes committed, welfare checks dispersed?

THE SOCIAL-CORPORATE MANAGEMENT GAP: HOW WIDE?

How practical is the application of proven business management techniques to the nation's social agencies and institutions? The basic differences between social and corporate management are well known. The overriding "profit" objective in a social institution is, or should be, improvement of the human condition. Thus traditional barometers of the profit and loss marketplace, used to rate "product acceptance," cannot be applied to determine how well a social program is accomplishing its purpose.

But significant similarities do exist in the planning, organization, and management of large-scale social and business endeavors. The managerial function of goal setting and the development of programs and actions designed to achieve the goals are processes common to both. Efficient resource allocation is as crucial to one as the other. Complex problems and decision requirements are generated by all ambitious enterprises and a well-structured information network is necessary if they are to be dealt with effectively.

Further similarities may be cited. Whether referred to as "population" or "public," "customers" or "clients," both social and business institutions have a market to serve and, presumably, to satisfy. No corporation would indiscriminately shrink or expand its market coverage, but would make such moves only after painful and comprehensive analysis to determine which segments might be served most effectively and profitably. Should a social organization settle for less?

Admittedly, the key indicators for testing assumptions, coping with change, and avoiding costly surprises would differ sharply for the profit and nonprofit sectors. But the management processes and techniques for developing them are essentially the same.

Business executives, their sensitivities honed to market and product-development opportunities, constantly use marketing research, technology transfer, and other sophisticated strategies to explore untapped potential. These techniques are just as available to social planners and managers who wish to develop new social products and programs for the benefit of the clients they serve.

The measurement of performance and results is as critical to the optimization of programs and elimination of waste in the social sector as it is in the business sector. Highly computerized monitoring systems, employed with great effectiveness by the aerospace industry and others, were applied extensively in the Apollo lunar landing program. In the opinion of some experts, the exceptional "visibility" created as a result was a major factor in the project's success.

The social-corporate management gap—the differences in abilities, techniques, and concepts required to manage effectively—is smaller than most people realize. The basic management skills of planning, organization, persuasion, human motivation, and development of human capabilities are common to all kinds of enterprise. Granted, the state of the art of business management is far from perfect in every dimension. And in some areas of the social sector, corporate managers have a great deal to learn from dedicated social planners in accenting human needs. But on balance, the reality is undeniable. Innumerable corporate survival techniques have been tested in the marketplace and proven on the earnings statement. Many of the time-honored techniques are applicable to social institutions and social programs. And yet in the great majority of cases they are not being applied. The failure to do so, I believe, is one of the greatest mistakes being made in society today. It's a mistake we can rectify starting tomorrow, using the strategies of Socio-Economic Management as a guideline for survival. Changing priorities is not enough.

OPERATION TURNAROUND

Though still relatively rare, attempts are being made to apply hard-won business know-how to social programs and problems. One such attempt is an experiment called Executive Interchange, a program in which executives from 31 major corporations swap jobs with government agency managers. A case in point is Thomas J. O'Brien, a noise abatement program manager for the Federal Aviation Administration. In 1970 he took a one-year leave of absence to function as a product line manager for Mobil Oil Corporation. Today, armed with a storehouse of business management experience, he's back at FAA in an exciting new systems and research job.

Under the middle management swap program, a North American Rockwell specialist, who helped prepare the B-1 bomber proposal, was assigned to the Office of Management and Budget where he developed a performance measurement system to assess various government social programs. A systems engineer from Bendix Corp. Aerospace Division worked in the transportation department on a tracked, air-cushion vehicle for mass transit. On the government's side, the Postal Service's director of systems analysis is working for AT&T as manager of management science research.

Experiments of this kind are exciting and encouraging. Unfortunately, with key managers displaced from important jobs, the interchange program may be fraught with problems and limited in scope.

Far less limited is the knowledge-transfer potential achievable by tapping the mental and technical resources of professional managers in a variety of disciplines. Business planners and analysts, marketing, research and financial executives, accountants and lawyers, human engineers and management development specialists have refined the skills of their trade to an impressive degree during recent decades.

The tragedy is that the bulk of this muscle and talent is not being applied to the treatment of our social ills. The problem has little to do with its availability. It is more a matter of attitude and style. As with other deeply rutted civilizations of ages past, our approach has become too narrow, too cautious, too conservative, and too imitative of yesteryear—even, perhaps, too "establishment."

Today we stand at the threshold of a new and historic era. What better time for the concerned citizen, the concerned official, the concerned social planner to sound a clarion call for help? Finding remedies for society's great needs is everyone's business.

Turning to the profit sector for counsel and guidance is both natural and logical. The area of measurement affords a prime example. Controllers and other financial executives charged with budgeting authority and responsibility regard the monitoring and measurement of performance and results as an indispensable funding tool. With the assistance of accountants, systems analysts, and industrial engineers, the art of measurement has been honed to a fine edge. It is in the interest of every citizen, whatever his profession, that the business-proven techniques of measurement be applied to the nonprofit sector. Only then can adequate social services be generated at a cost that will not bankrupt the nation. Too often in the past, social endeavors have been initiated and funded, refunded and perpetuated on a scattershot basis. We have now learned that the blind barrages simply do not work. We have the techniques and we know how to use them. It is time we did so.

The moment is ripe for Socio-Economic Management to establish itself on a nationwide front. And the attractiveness of the concept is that we need no special legislation, no drawn-out hearings, no involved studies or research undertakings to get the system under way. All we need is the will, the imagination, and the courage to switch from status quo to status go.

THE PRACTICAL APPLICATION

Socio-Economic Management, to repeat, is the application of business control principles and techniques to the measurement and analysis of the social and economic consequences of business and nonbusiness activities on the public sector—or more specifically, on people. In its broadest context, it would apply all the proven tools of business management to social institutions and programs.

SEM starts with established management basics. It begins with an objective, proceeds with a plan, shores the plan with commitment, and follows through by means of monitoring and measurement to a successful conclusion. If, anywhere along the line, the program starts to run off course, the system automatically sounds an alarm.

One of the chief causes of social program failure to date has been that too many management decisions have been made by social administrators who lack the training, experience, and skill to cope with the problem at hand. There's no more reason, for example, to expect a good funding judgment from a sociologist or economist than there would be to expect a reasoned sociological judgment from an accountant.

Management and accounting, incidentally, happen to be my own fields of endeavor and ones with which I am particularly well acquainted. I am thus more than ordinarily cognizant of the number of management and accounting judgments being made in our hospitals, universities, government agencies, and other social institutions by men and women with little if any management and accounting background and education.

In what capacity might a business executive serve the nonbusiness sector? Here, out of one of my own fields of experience, is a hypothetical example of how a professional accountant might participate in a poverty program under a system of Socio-Economic Management.

Setting: The Slumville section of Big City, U.S.A. The area consists mainly of dilapidated housing—dirty, rundown, rat-infested. It also contains a small factory employing 100 workers.

Objective: Operation Renewal. To rehabilitate Slumville, making it habitable and self-supporting.

Proposed Plan: To pass legislation permitting the government to purchase all real estate in Slumville, with both residents and factory to be relocated. All parties involved would be compensated for their property as well as the cost of relocation. The land would then be sold to private developers who would rebuild the area with modern homes and buildings.

Needless to say, several diverse professional management skills would play a role in a program of this scope: legal, general management, and others apart from the sociological, economic, urban, and political expertise required. But, zeroing in on specifics, let us deal for the time being with the accounting requirement in particular.

The accountant enters the picture early in the game in estimating the cost of the project and calculating real estate values in the area. He would also evaluate the cost of relocating the families and businesses displaced, and the cost of the agency that would be set up to run Operation Renewal. Deducted from these disbursements would be the income received from the sale of Slumville real estate to private developers. Included in the computations would be the increased tax produced by the added value of real estate holdings after renewal.

The accountant's function thus far appears simple enough and logical enough. It might well lead an outsider to ask: "Isn't this the way the job has always been done?"

The answer, unfortunately, is, "Too frequently, no." In many such programs, government costs have been calculated, not by accountants, but by economists, sociologists, or political scientists.

Innovative thinking of accountants would also be useful in other areas of Operation Renewal. Suppose, as so often happens, several of the 100 factory employees are relocated in a part of Big City considerably removed from the plant and that transportation to the company's new location is unavailable. If these workers are unable to find jobs near their new homes and draw unemployment compensation as a result, is this cost a part of the program?

Or if the relocated company cannot recruit enough employees at its new location, what costs are involved and who should bear them? And what about the people living outside Slumville who lose their jobs because of the factory's relocation? If they're unable to find new jobs and collect unemployment compensation as a result, how should these costs be calculated?

Even in modest social improvement programs, scores of problems arise. As part of the rehabilitation activity a Slumville school is razed and children bused to another school area. Should the busing be part of the rehabilitation cost? As a further result of rehabilitation, the traffic pattern is altered. Sections adjacent to Slumville are now cut off from direct access to thoroughfares and public transportation linking them to the business center. What role does this adverse effect play in the overall cost computation?

There is also housing to consider. What happens to the Slumville poverty dwellers who cannot obtain apartments at the low rental formerly paid? If they are forced to double up with other families, what price tag do you put on the discomfort involved? What kind of indicators do you set up? Who bears the brunt of the cost? And how?

What we have outlined here is just a small sampling of the factors so often ignored or overlooked in administering a program of social improvement. Relevant cost information is frequently lacking because measurement standards are either unavailable, ignored, or, where they do exist, misapplied.

REALLOCATING HUMAN RESOURCES

That the cost picture is garbled in so many cases is anything but surprising. It would be garbled in business as well if a sociologist or political scientist were called in to set up and administer a budget for a product development program.

The social institution is a political, economic, and sociological entity. It is also a complex organization that requires advanced professional management techniques if it is to operate effectively.

Everyone recognizes the critical role played by the sociologist, economist, political scientist, and agency administrator in the conception, planning, and management of a social improvement program. But however important they may be, these professionals could not do the job unassisted at the top decision levels any more than a group of accountants, lawyers, and general business managers could function in the nonprofit sector independent of the social planners.

Working together, however, in the same spirit of teamwork and cooperation that put a man on the moon, we can enter exciting new realms of achievement. This in a nutshell is what Socio-Economic Management is all about—interdisciplinary groupings to plan, control, and evaluate; SEM Councils; SEM audits.

6

THE
ORGANIZATION
OF SURVIVAL

No system of social change and reform, however well grounded and intelligently planned, can be superimposed on a framework of nonorganization, or chaos. Today's despotism in our society is one of institution versus man. Our business planners seem well aware of this harsh reality. Our social planners seem equally aware, but they take longer to get moving, perhaps because the wheels of government grind more slowly.

In *Future Shock,* Toffler states: "Today, organizational lines are changing so frequently that a three-month-old table [of organization] is often regarded as a historic artifact, something like the Dead Sea Scrolls." He goes on to quote McKinsey & Co. officer D. R. Daniel on the subject, and then former HEW Secretary John Gardner.

"My own observation as a consultant," says Daniel, "is that one major restructuring every two years is probably a conservative estimate of the current rate of organizational change among the largest industrial corporations."

Gardner asserts: "The farsighted administrator . . . reorganizes to break down calcified organizational lines. He shifts personnel. . . . He redefines jobs to break them out of rigid categories." Gardner also describes "crises of organization" in government and adds, "Most organizations have a structure that was designed to solve problems that no longer exist."

This gets to the heart of the matter. Gardner's message, concludes Toffler, amounts to a call for permanent revolution in organizational life, and more and more sophisticated managers are recognizing that in a world of accelerating change reorganization is, and must be, an ongoing process, rather than a traumatic once-in-a-lifetime affair.

If SEM strategies are to work, we must first lay an organizational foundation conducive to success. We must start with objectives.

Misguided and obsolete objectives lead to organizational decay. We tend to mistake form for substance, paperwork for action, numbers for needs. The moment an agency or program loses sight of its true objectives, it begins to deteriorate. The numbers and pieces of paper multiply while needs fulfillment shrivels.

In too many areas of social endeavor we have tended to lose sight of real objectives. We must retreat from numbers-based decisions and advance toward people-based decisions. Society as a whole and the individual organization it supports must adjust to the needs and values of its own time, or perish.

Evidence of organizational decay is all around us. The Department of Health, Education and Welfare is a prime example. Referred to as "Heartbreak House" by Senator Abraham Ribicoff, a former secretary of HEW, it is like a ten-ton albatross around the nation's neck. Shortly after Elliot Richardson stepped in to take over the formidable head job, the $76 billion octopal behemoth was described by *Fortune* writer Juan Cameron as "a monument to bureaucratic disorderliness." As Cameron went on to say,

A White House budget expert estimates that fully to fund programs already authorized in HEW alone would require a 16 percent increase in personal and corporate income-tax rates. And despite this fact of life Congress each year adds more programs, with little regard to the growing overlap, duplication, and confusion. . . . HEW has been compared to a slot machine that pays out money on hundreds of programs without any overall plan or assurance of equity. The Social Security Administration, which accounts for five-sevenths of HEW's budget and half of its employees, is essentially a highly mechanized checkwriting operation, independent of secretarial control in most respects. . . . Richardson, quite rightly, sees his chief problem to be gaining control of a large and rapidly growing budget, rather than plotting grandiose new policy departures from a disorderly base. . . . Twenty different programs, managed under fifteen sets of guidelines, support the education of the ghetto child. Under this system, Richardson says, it is hardly surprising that "we have not gotten the results we so confidently expected."

Mammoth though it may be, HEW represents just a piece of the chaos. One day in October 1969, the mayors of Boston, Pittsburgh, Detroit, Minneapolis, and Jackson, Mississippi met to discuss the problems of the cities, and characterized them as being perhaps even worse than they seem. As Jerome P. Cavanagh, the then mayor of Detroit, stated the case: "You have a fortuitous patchwork of New Deal programs, demonstration projects, things that were developed in the thirties, forties, fifties, some in the sixties. Until there's a commitment on the part of our national leadership to formulate a policy and goals, we're just going to continue to go down this crazy road we're on."

Jackson Mayor Allen C. Thompson, addressing himself to organization, commented wryly, "I'm not trying to be silly, but have you ever thought about dividing your cities up instead of making them bigger?"

NONORGANIZATION BREEDS INEFFICIENCY

Positive change and the social turnaround we seek are blocked on all fronts by bureaucracy, confusion, and decision paralysis. As we have seen, inefficiency, fostered by organizational chaos, tends to heap abuse on abuse.

Urgent as the need is for innovation and experimentation in our nation's institutions and agencies, nonorganization militates against success even when new ideas are tried. Analyzing the "war on poverty" and its various grants, author Richard W. Poston delves into the history of the Real Great Society. Manned by tough street kids, RGS was a New York gang organized to counter the detrimental effects of the city's juvenile warring factions. The idea lacked neither imagination nor originality, and it was backed by federal funds, Youth Organization United, and foundation money.

But, as Richard W. Poston puts it: "The gang leaders wanted recognition and independence with no strings attached. What they got was a passkey to never-never land. After being sufficiently romanticized, fawned upon, and showered with gifts, RGS was rendered incapable of dealing effectively even with itself." In time it deteriorated into "a kind of glorified payroll operation."

Little wonder. The program, it would appear, was defeated by organizational inefficiency before it began.

Almost invariably, the problem consists of ill-defined objectives compounded by a poor understanding of needs. As New York City budget director Frederick Hayes affirmed before a Senate subcommittee on the evaluation of social programs, we have almost no information at all on the way people feel about the most pressing problems of our society.

The way they perceive such problems, Hayes stressed, is at least as important in determining public pressure, as well as public apathy, as any amount of factual data. How many Americans truly believe that hunger is a crucial problem in this country? How many believe that crime is increasing far out of proportion to the actual impact of criminal activity on their own lives? No one really has the answers to questions of this kind.

Yet the questions could be answered. As Hayes points out, opinion sampling and other techniques for pinpointing human perceptions—and such pinpointing is vital if we are to achieve a meaningful restructuring of our agencies and social programs —long have been used successfully in both the profit and non-profit sectors. Commercial polling of the marketplace has become a science. In political polling, we have learned how to sample small population segments to arrive at highly, if not uncannily, accurate results. There's no reason to believe that these already tested and proven skills could not be applied to the planning that is required if our social endeavors are to be shaped in accordance with the equally proven precepts of Socio-Economic Management.

Yet we see a disquieting paucity of basic and applied research in areas that might lead to a more meaningful structuring of our social institutions. It is thus no surprise that programs and projects are being addressed to needs that are misconstrued and perceptions that are vague or outdated.

THE BLIGHT OF ANTIQUE LAWS

School systems profess to teach our children reading, writing, and arithmetic, but all too often—fettered by the habits and traditions of the past—they do not. City governments profess to administer urban areas in the best interests of their inhabitants, but all too often they do not. Police departments profess to protect the life and property of our citizens, but all too often they do not.

The reason all too often is organizational decadence, with environmental needs sacrificed to rigid organization and ruinous, outdated statutes. The artificial impediments to health care alone are stupendous. For one thing, diverse and highly fragmented state licensing of health practices thwarts the effective use of manpower—and the whole gamut of medical and paramedical specializations is involved. Nationwide, the administration of licensing laws is vested in hundreds of autocratically functioning regional boards. Some 794 statutes are involved, and the chief purpose behind many of them is to keep fiefdoms intact.

Clearly, as Blue Cross Association President Walter J. McNerney and other health leaders repeatedly urge, more is required than a mere chipping away at ancient and anachronistic laws. A total restructuring is in order, with licensing organized in accordance with community needs. This would bring consumers, businessmen, government officials, health professionals, and other specialists into the picture, working side by side on a multidisciplinary basis to strengthen, not individual empires, but a delivery system geared to human requirements.

BLUEPRINT FOR RESTRUCTURING

Organizations, like people, are susceptible to a number of ills that often go unrecognized until major surgery is required. These ills range from the unwieldy structuring, self-protectionism, and regulatory strictures already discussed, to the individual self-glorification and status quo adulation that flourish wherever organizational inadequacies exist.

Unquestionably, fixing responsibility and authority for weeding out unnecessary or stifling segments is at least as important as fixing responsibility and authority for enlarging an organization when the workload requires it. In practice, the human propensity for expanding operations leads administrators to build with alacrity. But when it comes to cutbacks or divestiture, it's a different matter. The more you control, the more important you are is a long-standing credo, and there are few administrators anxious to reduce their own importance. The reforms must come from outside the organization.

They must come in large part from those of us trained and disciplined in the techniques of analysis and the implementation of advanced management skills—not only accountants and consultants, but executive planners and organizational experts in all areas of enterprise. We owe it to society, to ourselves, and to the organizations we wish to preserve to extend our visions of responsibility beyond self-interest to the broader goal of survival—for if this society's turnaround effort should fail, where indeed would our self-interest lie?

The question is how and where we can participate. But first, of course, we must answer the question: What specifically needs to be done?

The chief executive of virtually any major corporation will have a ready answer to this question. The head of a conglomerate enterprise may even be more specific. And when you boil down the advice and suggestions, three key operational words are apt to emerge: *prune, divest,* and *merge.*

Diversified industrial corporations in particular learned during the "go-go" days of the late sixties that size for the sake of size alone usually generates more problems than solutions.

Social restructuring must be determined by scientific research and analysis and tailored to the prevailing situation. In countless sprawling agencies one or more segments function wastefully and ineffectively. In such cases, serious consideration should be given to closing down the nonproductive functions, turning them over to other agencies, or dividing the unwieldy organization into smaller, autonomous, more manageable units.

The principles of good organization apply no less to government agencies than they do to corporations.

To the experienced businessman, pruning, personnel realignment, divestiture, acquisition, and restructuring to boost performance is an old story. When a for-profit enterprise finds its executive hierarchy too old or inadequate, or finds that its capital needs exceed available lines of credit, or that its scope is too limited to take full advantage of its opportunities, a common solution is to make the organizational changes necessary to the strengthening of resources and achievement of goals.

Innumerable cases could be cited. In 1970, hampered by high interest costs, military cutbacks and a sluggish economy, Avco Corporation's stock plunged 60 percent while common stock dividends were suspended. A year later the company was able to report a lusty profit gain and distribution of a 65¢-per-share dividend. The turnaround was fueled largely by a well-thought-out organizational restructuring. Two divisions were merged for greater efficiency. An abrasives and household appliance division was spun off. A helicopter plant was shut down and the operation absorbed elsewhere.

When Allis-Chalmers found itself bogged down a few years ago in a morass of policy-making confusion, an organizational revamping of personnel was made to correct the situation. An "office of the president" was set up with three group vice-presidents eliminated. This removed the confusion of conflicting policies and decisions and gave all of management a better fix on the company's direction.

Some years back Donald C. Burnham took over at Westinghouse and found that company plagued by organizational problems that were causing program and decision bottlenecks. His solution was a reasoned restructuring that lopped off anemic parts of the operation and made other units more efficient. The program included cutbacks, acquisitions, management changes, and a variety of pruning moves. Its semiconductor business, console, television, stereo, vending machine operation, X-ray division, and other marginal profit makers were disposed of. Burnham is still at it today, pruning and chopping where necessary, merging and divesting to optimize corporate capabilities in line with well-defined profit objectives.

It gives one pause. Why must organizational renewal directly linked to profit-building goals be confined primarily to the commercial sector? Aren't government institutions supposed to make a profit too—a social profit? Why not, for example, an agency-set objective of 30 percent of welfare recipients gainfully employed by a specific date, and this goal accompanied by the restructuring needed to make it an achievable reality? Why, if a social agency is operating in the red—that is, failing to satisfactorily fulfill human needs—shouldn't organizational change be made mandatory?

THE SOCIAL SYNERGISTS

During the great merger era of the sixties the so-called synergistic formula for successful corporate marriage, $2 + 2 = 5$, appeared so often in the press it became a boring cliché. But that was apparently in business circles only. I cannot recall a single case of the formula being applied to a nonbusiness merger. Yet evidence proves that social mergers, when blessed by resources that dovetail and a good management "fit," can be every bit as fruitful as the most successful wedding.

Rehabilitation centers, poverty programs, colleges, and hospitals often stand to benefit by joining forces with others. Take the example of a community drug control center hastily established in response to pressing local needs and the efforts of a well-intentioned crusader or two. Later, after the building is up and fully equipped, it becomes clear that for economic or operational reasons, the center's progress is stymied. What too often happens in such cases is that the unit limps along from year to year, supported largely by public funds, but not really catering to the human needs it was set up to meet. In such a situation, wouldn't all involved benefit by a well-considered merger with a similar institution in order to serve the target population more effectively?

This has been done, in isolated instances, with outstanding success. The Arizona hospital merger of eight hospitals of varying size to form a greatly strengthened medical complex has already been cited. General Hospital of Kansas City, Missouri provides another good example.

For years it had been considered a "shambles" by civic leaders and the press. Then, one day about ten years ago, Nathan Stark, now chairman of Hallmark Cards, decided to do something about it. What he accomplished was an inspiring and instructive reorganization of the city's health care system that converted a trouble-plagued institution into a service- and needs-oriented health center. Today a variety of facilities, which include a psychiatric hospital, extended care center, dental school, children's hospital, state medical school and a health resources institute, have been united in a modern complex that serves as a model for health practitioners throughout the nation.

Stark, though he sparked and piloted the effort, would be the first to admit that he couldn't have done it alone. The reorganization was a concentrated multidisciplinary effort (a word increasingly associated with successful social ventures) that involved business and nonbusiness leaders in an active and meaningful way. "More and more these days," says Stark, "health care is becoming a melting pot of government and private enterprise."

And this is true not only of health care but of other social endeavors. The operation of the cities themselves is no exception.

While some areas of administration would benefit if the unwieldy behemoths they have become were broken down into manageable parts, in other areas the merging of resources would be beneficial. In Nashville, Tennessee, for example, Mayor Beverly Briley is especially proud of his success in consolidating county and city government for greater efficiency. "Prior to consolidation," he claims, "the business community was fed up. The downtown was dying and many of our leading businesses were preparing to leave." One black leader, Robert Lillard, who was vehemently opposed to consolidation from the outset, has since changed his mind. "I've seen much good come out of this," he told a reporter. "Economy and efficiency have improved, particularly the elimination of dual school systems and law-enforcement agencies."

In Indianapolis, the story was much the same. In 1969 Mayor Richard G. Lugar helped mobilize committees and task forces of businessmen, professionals, and other residents with special skills—another example of multidisciplinary planning and action that paid off to create a tighter and more efficient system.

NEW REMEDIES OR NEW EVILS?

Francis Bacon said it almost four centuries ago, but it applies as strongly today as it ever did: "He that will not apply new remedies must expect new evils."

One of the most powerful attributes of the dynamic, needs-oriented organization is its capability and willingness to explore and experiment. The value of innovation, of varying the input mix to improve the output, has long been appreciated in business. For a company to remain competitive in today's marketplace it must try, and keep trying, various combinations of advertising, packaging, research and development, production and distribution techniques, and other innovations. Each year we demand and get new models in cars and appliances, new fashions, new services in fields ranging from finance to recreation. But our schools, our lawmaking establishments, and our penal institutions remain largely unchanged.

Why shouldn't social institutions experiment as business does with a variety of inputs in an effort to favorably alter the quality and cost of meeting public needs? We have been doing too many things wrong in our society for too long a time. Doing more of the same will not solve our problems. Health care, as always, provides the classic example.

"Are we spending money for the wrong kind of care?" That's a question posed by WCBS-TV science editor Earl Ubell.

If the critics are right, the new [health] insurance programs, if passed, will serve mainly to drive up demand for health care— which will in turn drive up costs, thereby consuming a substantial portion of our national talent and treasure—and there will be little improvement in the mortality and morbidity statistics to show for it. The alternatives: Put more effort into traditional areas of nutrition, housing and sanitation, especially among the poor. And break new ground with nonmedical preventive measures—campaigns for auto and home safety, massive anti-cigarette, anti-alcohol, anti-drug programs, and high-powered educational schemes to teach us to take care of ourselves.

He is talking about innovation.

The need for innovation in our social institutions grows more pressing every day. Modern organization must be capable, not only of responding to change, but of initiating it. It must be able to shift human and physical resources from areas of low productivity to areas of significant performance. It must stop what is wasteful and replace it with what is fruitful.

An abundance of evidence bespeaks the high potential in areas where meaningful change is applied. Law enforcement, an especially thorny area, is no exception. In Washington, D.C., for example, innovative police chief Jerry V. Wilson, drawing upon a special fund, has launched a system of immediate bonuses for outstanding performance—rapid response, quick and thorough identification of suspects, good follow-up in gathering facts for successful prosecution. He tells subordinates: "You don't control an organization through orders. Men respond to what they see an organization wants."

Another Wilson program is called "You Can Help." Here citizens are encouraged to call in information about suspected crimes, and an avalanche of information has come in. Calls have rocketed from 4,500 per day pre-Wilson to a current daily average of 7,000. Other experiments in Washington are meeting with like success. The police chief's philosophy is simple: "How well you can come up with the mix of responses is the measure of how well you do the job."

Imaginative police action is also reported from Indianapolis. In a park one day last spring, young people were angered by police activity stemming from complaints about young sex deviates and open drug use. A confrontation between police and long-haired youngsters, most of whom were nonoffenders, appeared unavoidable. As the hostile teenagers awaited police arrival, ice cream trucks driven by casually dressed young men rolled up to the scene. The drivers proceeded to hand out ice cream, and, following this, footballs. Soon several games of touch football were under way. It gradually dawned on the young people, as well as the crowd that had gathered in anticipation of a major clash, that the drivers were not ice cream vendors, but police officers with experience in local youth programs.

There is no reason why similar innovation couldn't be extended to all areas of social action. As enthusiastic fans of our free enterprise system are fond of reminding us, there's no nation on earth that can match the United States when it comes to applying imagination and ingenuity. We can turn out ideas in abundance, and ideas are what made America great. And now, more than ever, we need new ones—and need to apply them.

For too long our poverty programs have been largely locked into doling out food, clothing, and shelter without addressing themselves to the real underlying need—helping the ghetto poor to work themselves out of the hopeless bind they're in.

Why not take a hard new look at this nation's entire judicial system? Virtually every lawyer, court clerk, and judge in the country knows that the need for innovation that will speed the administration of justice grows more critical daily. It is so crucial, in fact, that Chief Justice Warren Burger has urged legal experts to brainstorm for fresh ideas—not to worry whether they work perfectly or even whether they are constitutional, but to strike out in new directions and leave the details for later.

One legal panel, the Special Advisory Group on Federal Civil Litigation, headed by New York University law professor Robert A. Leflar, recently submitted its first recommendations: Abolish jury trials in condemnation proceedings to obtain land for federal projects. Fine lawyers for time-wasting practices during court sessions. Create special courts for antitrust and other trade regulation cases. Bar appeals (now an absolute right in federal trials) in cases involving Social Security claims and other special categories. Replace regional courts of appeal with a single, national, middle-level federal court.

And in many federal and state courts across the nation attempts are being made to pare the sacred 12-man jury to a more manageable six. This is already being done in several states.

Why not take a realistic new look at our educational system and create training opportunities tailored to needs? Certainly centuries-old traditional methods are being challenged on all fronts today.

Author–educator Ivan Illich is convinced that "only a radical redistribution of education can enlarge human freedom of mind, spirit, and talent." To eliminate the "social addiction" to attending school, he proposes a de-schooled world that would replace most formal classes with networks of "learning exchanges." Instead of confining the young in schools, which he contends only prolong childhood, such exchanges would integrate all generations. Encouraged by tax incentives, businesses could employ interested children between the ages of eight and 14 "for a couple of hours each day if the conditions were humane." People of any age who wanted to learn something would go to a counselor somewhat as they would to a reference librarian.

Far out? Perhaps. But it may not seem so a generation or two from today. And the trend of current advanced thinking seems to point in that direction. A special task force chaired by Frank Newman, Stanford University's associate director of university relations, has drawn up a whole battery of educational reform proposals at the behest of HEW. Among the new ideas:

• A kind of G.I. Bill of Rights for "service to people." This would reward any legitimate work—paid or volunteer—in local, state, or national activities of the community service kind with financial credits toward college tuition.

• Federal scholarships to legitimize interrupted study. This would help to unlock the traditional four-year unit.

• Establishment of regional advisory centers for students. These are desperately needed to overcome the inadequate guidance counseling in most high schools.

• Creation of a telecommunications center. This would permit faculty members who are interested in putting their work on tape, screen, or computer to undergo rapid training by production experts in these areas.

Why not? The need for innovation was never more urgent nor the time more ripe.

A BASE FOR BUILDING

This chapter must end as it began. Program innovation and all social reform must stem from a strong and solid foundation. Smear a fresh coat of paint on a rusty surface, and the rust will not take long to reappear.

We require restructured agencies to achieve our social goals because in too many cases the ones we have cannot do the job. Social institutions, more often than not, are too fragmented, unwieldy, and snarled by bureaucratic red tape to respond with vigor and imagination to the problems they were organized to tackle.

Sensitive to the urgency of the situation, and cognizant of the effectiveness of proven business techniques, President Nixon has repeatedly urged corporate leaders and problem-solving specialists to help root out inefficiencies and initiate reforms. The progress to date has been unimpressive except in isolated cases. This has not been because the talent and expertise were overestimated or because the desire and readiness to pitch in are lacking, but primarily because the nonorganizational base has been left intact. In a number of instances, new paint has been applied. But the rust is rarely removed.

Bureaucratic rust tends to develop from within. It encourages the building and preservation of fiefdoms and sanctifies the status quo.

The evidence can be seen most clearly in our larger cities. Many of them first evolved as independent oases of urban life, in the midst of rural countryside, or along a barren coastline. Institutions to govern were created on an ad hoc basis and expanded gradually. While these organizational structures became rigid, the surrounding area grew in population and industrial facilities so that today the geographical boundaries of a city like New York no longer have much significance. The areas surrounding the central city—northern New Jersey, southern Connecticut, and so forth—have fused to become one massive megalopolis.

Yet the governmental organizations involved, still geared to outdated requirements, try to perpetuate their traditional roles. It just cannot work. Economic and social realities in urban areas no longer fit within the niches prescribed by antiquated local agencies. The inevitable disaster, so often referred to as the "crisis of our cities," is thus not surprising.

Nor is the crisis confined to city government. It embraces all categories of endeavor in the nonprofit sector, from education and health to transportation and a fair deal for the aged.

When angry young people on our nation's campuses—and on campuses throughout the world—attack the "establishment," they are merely expressing their disdain for the calcified organizations that have forgotten the purposes for which they were intended and failed in their responsibility to respond to basic human needs. These institutions have both proliferated and grown fat by feeding on themselves, one department busily shuffling papers that a second department self-importantly has ground out, while a third myopically takes to the filing cabinets in a futile attempt to keep up with the flood.

Yet the outlook is not all that gloomy. Government and non-government leaders—officials, administrators, businessmen, scientists, academicians, accountants, and other professionals—from virtually every field, forthright and imaginative men and women, have pinpointed the problem and are chafing to help revamp the system.

As Yale President Kingman Brewster, a leading spokesman for reform, makes clear,

In the area of institutional design and innovation we must rise to the challenge of the need for neighborhood, community, metropolitan institutions which are more humanly responsive than traditional political bureaucracies, and more locally rooted in the communities they serve than are the traditional professional service organizations. The neighborhood corporation, the community health center, the storefront legal assistance bureau, the housing rehabilitation workshop are merely suggestive. More intellectual imagination and more professional ingenuity is needed to shape institutions which encourage the fact and the feeling of community self-help and self-determination.

In some areas—health, education, city government, and others—the stirrings have begun to be felt. Here and there inspired crusaders have made exciting inroads. Some pruning, some merging, some divestiture, and some encouraging organizational innovation are already taking place. But don't let the publicity fool you. The experiments make news. The unruffled mass of stagnation that persists in one of the great afflictions of our time.

The process of reform on the whole has been painful and slow. What we have witnessed to date amounts to little more than a ripple on a semistagnant pond. The tenets and models of Socio-Economic Management herein contained could help to enlarge that ripple into a wave.

7

MARKETPLACE
STRATEGIES

Two major problems face top management in every commercial enterprise: (1) How can we motivate employees to generate maximum productivity? (2) How can we motivate consumers to buy our products and services?

It has long been recognized that successful motivation is crucial to corporate earnings. In recent decades an especially great amount of time, effort, and money have been invested in attempts to devise new incentive techniques designed to get a jump on the competition. A McGraw-Hill survey of 166 large companies in 31 industries reveals that 75 percent have regular bonus or incentive compensation plans and that 82 percent give stock options.

Xerox, Studebaker-Worthington, Warner-Lambert Pharmaceutical Co., and many other corporations go in for sophisticated incentives to keep managers producing at high performance peaks. One example is their practice of matching qualified stock options with phantom stock awards. The executive can exercise his option. Or he can take the amount of the appreciation between grant and exercise date in cash or stock. The 3M Company and others add a dazzling "Yo-Yo option" to their stock plans. Under this scheme, the executive's option price is lowered one dollar every time the company's stock price goes up one dollar.

As experience proves, such heady inducement pays off. At Mariott Corporation, where an outstanding record of 20 percent compounded annual growth has been chalked up over the past ten years, 8 percent of pretax profits go into a profit-sharing plan for employees. Gannett Co.'s highly successful newspaper empire paid out $625,222 worth of incentive money to 85 of its top executives in 1971.

Nor are motivational ploys confined in-house. To lure customers to its hotels and restaurants, Mariott chops markets into narrow customer segments and tailors its services to individual tastes, much in the way such sophisticated marketers as Procter & Gamble and Lever Bros. handle soap.

The trick that has worked for Gannett, according to Vice-President Warren McClure, has been to keep experimenting with new market incentive techniques and applying the ones that work to every newspaper in the chain. One such idea: Getting more dollars from each inch of advertising by charging a 25 percent premium for a position next to the comics or weather. If there is no space available on the comic page? Make the comics smaller.

A simple suggestion. But it may well come as a revelation to scores of newspapers, largely family-operated and controlled, where innovation has been an unfamiliar word for decades, just as it has been in a host of nonprofit organizations.

THE NEED FOR INCENTIVES

Though often devoted to their work, and in many cases less materialistic than corporate executives, social managers are just as human. And the users of social services are every bit as human as the users of commercial products; they are, in fact, the same individuals.

The evidence is that virtually all human beings will respond to motivation properly applied. Incentives that work in business—whether financial or job- or status-oriented—will work equally well in the public sector. But we have to apply them.

This we are not doing to any appreciable extent. The civil service is a prime example. "Instead of a merit system," writes E.S. Savas, first deputy commissioner in New York City's Office of the Mayor, "there is a seniority system. Promotions occur incestuously from within, based on examinations that attempt—but fail—to measure performance. . . . The able and devoted civil servant—and there are many—is often no better rewarded than the incompetent slacker and finds himself vilified by the public for the negligence and lethargy of his colleagues."

What happens to people when motivation is missing? A relative handful are self-motivated by their desire to change, to reform, to contribute. But unfortunately such individuals, however inspiring their spirit, remain in the minority. The majority of us, unspurred by incentives, tend to give in to apathy and indulge in rationalization.

In a penetrating analysis of national priorities, a distinguished group of Brookings Institution economists makes the point that "the multiplication of dollars and programs brought not solutions for such problems as welfare reform, day care, and city finance but a multiplication of problems." Money, they stress, is no more the answer than a numerical increase of efforts. How could it be when the federal payout for social programs has rocketed from $30 billion to $110 billion in ten years?

What the Brookings group presses for is the kind of precise, clinical experimentation that is more than a mask for inaction. "They have their own preferred approach," writes *New York Times* columnist Jack Rosenthal. "Instead of trying to promote change through the force of regulation, they say, more emphasis should be given to incentives. For example, instead of forbidding water pollution, they contend it would be more effective to levy clean-up charges on companies that continue to dump waste in rivers."

Do we possess the know-how and expertise to produce innovation of this kind on a broad national basis? Professor Robert N. Anthony of the Harvard Business School states, "Many of the techniques developed in the private sector are useful in nonprofit organizations, but they have been slow to adopt them." Acknowledging that the driving force in our economy is competition, he adds:

Much can be done to promote a spirit of competition within a nonprofit organization. In the Navy, for example, the several Navy shipyards now compete with one another for business. They bid for overhaul work and if their price is not low enough or the service not good enough to obtain a satisfactory volume of the overhaul work, this is a signal that something is wrong with the shipyard. A direct result of this competition was the shutting down of the Brooklyn Naval Shipyard.

This concept could easily be extended to other types of social enterprise. Under a competitive social system, hospitals, prisons, universities, and other institutions would earn funding points based on scientific projections of achievement, with performance periodically monitored to match results with commitments. Organizations failing to meet human needs effectively would be restructured, merged into more efficient operations, or shut down.

INCENTIVES IN ACTION

Albert Einstein once said that imagination is more important than knowledge. And Jules Verne remarked that whatever one man is capable of conceiving, other men will be able to achieve.

In America it has been proved repeatedly that imagination leads to knowledge, and knowledge leads to the solution of complex problems. We are a nation of conceptualists and, when we are able to debureaucratize the environment, a nation of achievers. Surely U.S. world leadership in management science and technology stems largely from our ability to attack major problems with creative ingenuity. In fact, "American ingenuity" long has been a byword of the historians who chronicle the origins and growth of our free enterprise system.

Does America possess the conceptual and implementational capabilities to introduce into our social institutions the marketplace incentives that are essential if we are to stave off disaster? The answer would appear to be yes, because scores of promising innovative plans have been and are being put into effect in a variety of nonprofit endeavors.

Most of the ideas are exciting. Some have been highly successful, some only partly so. Others are conceptually sound, but have been stymied by bureaucratic opposition, the stubborn resistance of little men defending little fiefdoms. Others fail because they are inadequately monitored and improperly controlled.

What follows is a small, representative sampling of incentive experiments designed by imaginative social planners. Here are specific actions that, starting tomorrow, could be expanded on a national basis to upgrade the quality of public service and American life. I do not mean to imply that these particular experiments are the panacea for our social ills, but they are the kind of experiments referred to by the Brookings Institution group and a host of other anti–status-quo thinkers.

While degree of dedication may vary from person to person and occupation to occupation, doctors, teachers, law enforcement officials, and social workers along with consumers, tenants, and social "clients" are really not all that different from employees of giant corporations. We all require motivation of one kind or another to inspire us to excellence. And whatever the pursuit, we need incentives to counter the temptations of laziness, mediocrity, and indifference.

Education

The year-round school. Innumerable public schools today are overcrowded, operating on double shifts, and poorly equipped. This was precisely the situation in 1970 in the communities of Valley View District 96, about 35 miles from Chicago. With over 6,900 grade-schoolers crammed into space for 5,280, and student growth of 500 to 600 a year projected, the situation had reached crisis proportions.

At emergency Board of Education and community meetings, alternatives were proposed out of sheer desperation: To crowd 50 to 60 children into each classroom, or to set up a system of half-day sessions. Their emotions near the boiling point, indignant parents vehemently rejected these proposals. But what course was left? This predominantly blue-collar community already was severely overtaxed financially.

With necessity breeding invention, a new alternative was found: the year-round school, or "45-15 Plan." Under the arrangement, students were to attend school 45 class days, then be off for 15 class days, or 21 to 25 actual days of vacation. This meant an extended vacation during each of the year's four seasons. Yet at the end of the year, the plan adds up to the customary 180 days of school attendance.

Despite the inevitable opposition of some teachers and parents, the plan was adopted. Experience proves it is educationally sound and contains undeniable benefits to the community. For one thing, it accommodates one-third more children in existing facilities. According to Valley View Superintendent Kenneth L. Hermansen, the district has saved the cost of two new buildings with 60 classrooms—about $6 million, including interest on 20-year bonds, plus 2 to 4 percent in operating costs.

Where do the incentives come in? The plan apparently works —despite minor opposition—because of the motivations involved. Most children love it. For them it means four long vacations each year instead of a long boring summer. For many parents, the headache of how to keep the youngsters occupied for almost three months has been eliminated, and as some point out: "We can now take vacation trips during any season of the year we prefer."

What about the teachers? Most of them enthusiastically endorse the 45-15 Plan. Given the option to work 180 days at a starting salary of $7,750 or 240 days at a starting salary of $10,300, all male teachers elected to work a full year. This relieved the financial pressures that plague most teachers and ended the need for moonlighting, which can only result in improved morale and higher quality performance. It also meant many byproduct benefits: reduced summer police problems, and money saved on summer programs designed to keep children occupied and off the streets.

Some of the questions raised by the Valley View experiment are obvious. Why wait for impending financial collapse before tackling the problem of school overcrowding and split-shift teaching prevalent in so many U.S. communities? Crisis management, even where creative ideas are implemented, is much less efficient than good long-range planning. Why shut down educational facilities worth billions of dollars for almost 25 percent of the year? What business enterprise could survive if its office and plant were to stand idle each year for so long a period?

And why hasn't action been taken to bring this plan, or modifications of it, into active consideration in communities from coast to coast? Within the past few months I have mentioned the Valley View experiment to at least a dozen educators of my acquaintance. Only four of them knew of the plan. Only two understood it in depth. Not one could state that the plan had been evaluated within his own community.

The three-year degree. "The notion of a four-year degree is a historical accident," states Alden E. Dunham of the Carnegie Corp. Would a three-year degree serve society better? It might. It might not. We will never know for sure unless it is properly tried, properly monitored, properly evaluated.

In 1971 the Carnegie Commission on Higher Education concluded, after a comprehensive study, that "the length of time spent in undergraduate education can be reduced roughly by one-fourth without sacrificing educational quality." St. Louis University, Ripon College, and others already offer three-year degrees, aimed at attracting more students and paring alarming deficits. Yale, Dartmouth, De Pauw, and other major schools are debating the move. Again, the main impetus for such evaluation is that so many institutions large and small are tottering on the rim of financial ruin. Another case of crisis management.

Shouldn't all educational institutions, high schools as well as colleges, be considering such a move—including those that are not yet perilously close to bankruptcy? For one thing, if successful, it would be a way of extending market options in the educational field, and this would be all to the good. It is in the nature of competition to eliminate what is disadvantageous and cause what is beneficial to flourish.

The benefits of the three-year degree are clear. It would save the undergraduate and his family $4,000 to $5,000, reduce the tax burden for millions, permit hundreds of schools to survive —and perhaps be more effective.

Desanctification of traditional concepts. "By doing business as usual," says William Jellema, research director of the Association of American Colleges, "private colleges have a life expectancy of zero years."

At least one private college, Southern California's La Verne, has decided to scrap traditional concepts of the teacher-oriented, high-cost curriculum. Says President Leland Newcomer: "We are junking the assumption that, if a student is to learn, he must be taught." The new approach is to give the student sufficient autonomy to plot his own educational course, with the faculty providing more guidance than participation. Since faculty salaries constitute the largest slice of the financial pie, and with fewer teachers needed under this system, economies should be substantial. At La Verne, once a perennial runner of deficits, economies have been sufficient to take the school out of the red.

For students who attend college to learn, the undisciplined approach can be intriguing and morale is described as high. Other schools add disincentives to the motivational mix. Hampshire College in Massachusetts has done away with tenure for its professors. It is thus not the captive of nonproductive teachers or inflexible curriculums, as so many schools are. Obviously, the instructor who is more concerned with publishing or consulting than teaching, or too lazy to vary and update his course to keep it exciting and alive, could not survive in this environment. At Livingston College in New Jersey, a part of Rutgers, students are permitted to sign up for courses, sit in on a couple of sessions, and switch if they are disappointed in the fare. A dull and dreary droner might thus wind up with an empty classroom—a powerful spur to increased teaching effort and, in essence, a marketplace technique.

Marketplace inputs of this type understandably are not too popular with some teachers, who worry that accountability and enforced standards of performance might compel them to work harder or cost them their jobs. Such feelings are common, of course, in both the public sector and the private—with one significant difference. In the private sector maintaining a reasonable level of achievement is an obvious condition of survival. In the public sector, historically at least, this has not been the case. But in the educational community, with the specter of bankruptcy staring so many administrators in the face, top men are beginning to wonder. In a shopper's market, shouldn't the primary consideration be to satisfy the customer?

Housing
Housing allowances. Federal government subsidies for low and middle income housing are creeping steadily toward the $2 bil-

lion mark. But the scope of the outlay provides no guarantee that subsidized projects will be maintained on a livable basis.

Now a program launched by the Department of Housing and Urban Development in an effort to correct this situation is under way in six cities.

Under the program qualified families receive a housing payment that may double the amount they normally could spend. With this they shop for their housing in the open market. Proponents see many advantages. Tenants get a wider choice where to live. They can move without losing their subsidy, as at present. This, it is hoped, will encourage landlords to maintain buildings. It would encourage greater use of existing housing in the nation's cities, something many experts believe makes more sense than building more expensive new construction. It would eliminate housing built especially for the poor and help avoid concentrations of the poor in certain neighborhoods. Finally, on a per-family basis, the cost of allowances would be substantially less. HUD Assistant Secretary Harold B. Finger estimates the costs of present subsidies could be cut in half. Or, twice as many people as today could be helped for the same money, a considerable advantage considering that some 25 million families, or 40 percent of the population, are eligible for housing subsidies.

Educational vouchers are based on the same conceptual approach. They permit clients to shop around and determine for themselves where their needs are met best, precisely as a buyer would do in purchasing a TV set, a vacation trip, or an automobile.

Tenant participation. Industrial marketers and researchers long have recognized the value of sounding out potential customers in an effort to zero in on true needs and desires and thus insure product acceptance. In the social sector to date, examples of "customer" consultation have been rare. Where it has been practiced, however, some dramatic results have occurred.

Sursum Corda is a low- and moderate-income housing project in Washington, D.C. Toward the end of the sixties, well in advance of the project's completion date, a tenant association was formed, with community leaders elected to its board. Tenants were asked to list the things they wanted most (they put washer-dryers first, air conditioners next). These they got—

along with terraces, freezers, landscaped courtyards, well-equipped recreational areas, and other amenities.

But such items come high, and with about half the tenants receiving federal assistance, cost limitations were rigid. So the icing was made available by sacrificing part of the cake. To get what they wanted, most tenants were willing to accept smaller rooms and unplastered cement block walls. They also gave up basements in their low-rise dwellings.

As any experienced industrial marketing executive might have predicted, listening to the customer paid off. At Sursum Corda, there is less than 5 percent turnover and few families have moved into the income range where the federal aid supplement is needed. Not that the road has been strewn with roses; serious problems dealing with protection in a high-crime area, booming maintenance costs, underestimates of the number of children in the development, and other hurdles had to—and still have to—be met and overcome. But the area is kept neat and clean, tenants take pride in their homes, and the far-lower-than-average rate of turnover is evidence that people are happy there.

Sursum Corda is a hopeful sign of the potential involved when the marketplace is given prime consideration in serving public needs. It is indicative of a growing trend, the acceleration of which would help to insure survival. Why not refine and expand this concept to include other social services on a national basis? Why not set up multidisciplinary decision-aiding groups in every community, consisting of trained professionals as well as representatives of the area being served? The function of these task forces would be to determine real needs and desires with regard to crime and drug control, recreation, health care, job training, youth centers, and the rest.

It is another important way of "shopping the market" before designing the product. It's a way of funding social programs in response to human requirements, not timeworn traditions, last year's statistics, or political expediency.

Jobs

Jawboning undoubtedly helps to some degree in getting reluctant businessmen to assume social responsibility. But stockholder pressures to sustain profit margins are usually more insistent. And all too often, the chief executive who listens more to his conscience than to the owners of his company places his neck dangerously close to the ax. So while jawboning helps, realistic incentives help even more.

With this in mind, the National Alliance of Businessmen (NAB), headed in 1972 by Gordon M. Metcalf, chairman of Sears, Roebuck and Co., embarked on a federally supported program to give companies a tax credit (20 percent of wages) for hiring individuals off the welfare rolls and training them to become self-sufficient.

Costly though such programs are, the alternative—the galloping giveaway binge—is obviously far more expensive from both an economic and human standpoint.

Health care

The needs of the disadvantaged have been well aired. Unpublicized, but just as real, are the needs of more fortunate citizens.

Doctors are no exception. It has been estimated by the American Medical Association, which has been unable to come up with a solution, that 132 U.S. counties, with a total of a half-million residents, are without doctors. The problem, some experts claim, is not so much a doctor shortage as it is maldistribution.

The typical medical practitioner has invested eight or more years of his life in arduous training. His family has invested many thousands of dollars to buy him an education. When his formal schooling is over and he sets up his practice, if he is at all conscientious he will continue studying eight or more hours per week to keep abreast of the latest developments. Having put this much time, money, and sweat into his career, the physician—at least according to his way of thinking—has some real needs of his own.

He needs to practice his profession in a professional environment. He needs access to modern and well-kept facilities. Obviously, cleanliness and sanitation are important to him. In addition, he needs reasonably convenient access to cultural centers, recreational activities, and friends and associates on an intellectual level comparable to his own. And he needs to be safe in his work and his play.

These things simply are not available in the ghettos of Harlem, or Newark, or Watts. Nor are they available in Horny Ridge, Montana.

It is safe to venture a guess that proportionately there are more very highly dedicated physicians—so dedicated to the services of humanity that individual style of life has become secondary—than there are very highly dedicated bus drivers, computer operators, and traveling salesmen. Nonethelesss, it is equally safe to guess that self-sacrificing practitioners are rare in any occupation, medicine included.

How, then, does one persuade doctors to practice in this nation's ghettos and outlying rural districts, where the lack of professional health care is acute? A host of schemes—mainly financial lures in the form of loans or grants—have been tried unsuccessfully. Little wonder. Money is not a prime incentive for most physicians, not because they don't like it, but because these days a good doctor can become affluent wherever he decides to set up practice. So why should he work in dismal surroundings, often in ill-equipped and poorly maintained facilities, in an area where culture, recreation, good restaurants, and other amenities are missing, and where he also has to worry about his safety?

A motivational expert in a large corporation might have an interesting approach to this problem. Ruling out money, he would explore and uncover other vital needs. Physicians, like most professional people, are concerned about professional status. Why not a system of credits, distinguished service awards so to speak, that would win national recognition—perhaps HEW citations, with special certificates and plaques to go with them—for part-time service in ghetto communities?

Research is important to many doctors. Since they often lack the access to research facilities, why not award research grants to physicians who serve part time in undesirable areas where they are critically needed?

What about quick and easy transportation that would whip doctors in and out of communities where they serve part time, eliminating the parking problem and exposing them to less physical danger? What about special paid leaves of absence to take special courses and advanced training as another service lure? And what about more sponsorship programs under which young men and women who could not otherwise afford medical educations would be government-supported providing they commit themselves for X number of years to ghetto or rural service?

The problem of health care distribution is a thorny one, to be sure. But as industry has learned through necessity, where needs can be identified, men and women can be motivated. And doctors have needs of their own.

Ecology

Recycled waste. Environmentalists long have lamented the mountainous volume of paper, metals, textiles, glass, wood products, and other waste materials polluting the environment. One important part of the solution to this problem, the experts agree, is the recycling and reuse of solid waste. Yet to date at least, government tax, transportation, and other controls make it unprofitable to use recycled items.

As one ecologist states the problem: "We need some new and imaginative ways to make recycled materials competitive with virgin materials." Referring to powerful industry lobbies, he adds more bluntly, "Of course, when you boil it down, you get rid of pollution by getting rid of the politics involved."

Spurred by mounting public pressures, some members of Congress are being stirred to action. At last reading, the Environmental Protection Agency had some measures in the works and was examining others. A variety of incentives have been proposed: Pare depletion allowances on virgin materials, government subsidization or purchase of recycled items, lower freight rates applied to recycled products, investment tax credits for the purchase of recycling equipment, and others.

All of these ideas have potential. But thus far lobbyists representing producers of virgin materials have held onto the reins. Slightly more than one-fifth of recyclable paper waste, for example, the major source of solid waste pollution, is now being processed, according to a Battelle Memorial Institute study. With the proper incentives applied, this story could be far more encouraging in a short period of time.

Pollution charges. Disincentives are sometimes more effective than positive motivations. The concept of pollution charges, needless to say, is highly controversial, since no businessman reacts kindly to a higher cost of doing business.

But here again, as pollution continues to devastate the environment and as social pressures mount, the trend is in favor of remedial action. According to *Business Week,* Senator William Proxmire, a long-time supporter of pay-to-pollute legislation, is pressing for a national plan that would levy a 10¢-per-pound charge as measured by the biochemical oxygen demand that effluents place on waterways. Revenues from pollution charges would help cities finance plans and facilities designed to clean up the environment.

Equally important would be the psychological implications relating to disincentives of this type. Pollution penalties would automatically motivate managers to cut pollution through improved production processes, new control technology, and recycling. As controls became effective, and effluents decreased, polluting companies could apply for fee reductions.

The newly created Council on Environmental Quality has come out in favor of pollution charges, a hopeful sign. Experience to date, though limited, is highly encouraging. A Springfield, Missouri, packing plant, the CEQ reports, was faced with a municipal waste-treatment charge of $1,400 per month. Motivated by this disincentive, it modified its process sufficiently to reduce the monthly payment to $225. And in Otsego, Michigan, a large industrial user cut its daily discharge dramatically —first, from 1,500 pounds of biochemical oxygen demand from the municipal waste-treatment system to 900 pounds when a pollution charge was levied, and then, 90 days later, to 500 pounds per day.

City Finances
With few exceptions, major U.S. cities from Bangor, Maine, to San Diego are in desperate financial straits. State aid, we hear, is one solution; federal aid is another. But when you boil it down, such aid is just another way of passing the cost burden along to the already overburdened taxpayer. A third alternative, barely explored or applied to date, is the levying of user charges in such a way as to allocate the cost load more equitably between users and nonusers of specific municipal services.

The user charge is an attractive way to finance new municipal programs and facilities. For one thing, it effectively measures consumer demand, providing planners with a gauge for use in expanding or cutting back on specific services. For another, it serves to balance the outlays for capital facilities and auxiliary gear. The imposition of user fees for such things as municipal tennis courts would offer new, more widespread incentives for excellence to municipal officials eager to boost revenues through increased user participation.

THE MS FACTOR

"MS" stands for the "management of success." It might also be interpreted to read the "multiplication of success." Permit me to hypothesize.

Suppose that an experimental system of small fees imposed by City A for the use of fishing, beach, tennis, and other recreational facilities produces sufficient income to fund desperately needed vital services and prevents the city's financial structure from breaking down. Or that a year-round school experiment in City B, after careful testing and evaluation, is found to exceed the community's most ambitious expectations. Or that a three-year-degree offering succeeds in making Migraine College financially independent for the first time in a decade or more. Or that "housing allowances" distributed to citizens of Bleak Ghetto quite obviously work to make housing in the area more competitive, thereby upgrading the level of quality and service. Or that an incentive plan offering doctors research or hospital privilege credits motivates physicians to practice part time in hitherto unserviced ghetto or rural communities.

What then?

Two simple and obvious conclusions may be drawn: First, that the problems experienced in these test communities were similar to problems experienced in scores of other communities across the nation; and second, that the strategy that works for one community will—with proper tailoring—work for other communities as well.

Why, then, aren't this nation's significant successes widely duplicated? Quite obviously—to draw on a number of basic

SEM precepts—the planning, organizational, coordinating, monitoring, and implementational machinery for achieving the MS factor has not been set in motion. As a result, a vast amount of potential for improvement is not being utilized.

Technology transfer

The key to the proper management and multiplication of success lies in a concept that increasing numbers of large corporations are adopting these days and referring to as "technology transfer," or by some similar label. In many companies special departments are established specifically for the purpose of investigating new ideas, new concepts, new technology, and for finding places within the corporation where they might most suitably be applied.

Technology transfer in the highly diversified company covers a wide scope of operations, both internal and external. One objective is to document profitable innovations made by one department or division and see to it that others in the company who might benefit by the thinking done, research conducted, or skills developed and experience garnered will have access if the profit opportunity warrants.

North American Rockwell, for example, has a highly sophisticated technology transfer operation in force. In such multifaceted and multidivisional operations, major subsidiaries often work autonomously. Without such a system, innovations developed within a division would be apt to go unnoticed by other divisions. One illustration of the practical value of technology transfer is the Nadyne concept for electrical alternators and motors created by NAR's Los Angeles Aerospace & Systems Group. A few features of this concept are the removal of brushes, the ability to operate at very high rotor speeds, and the feasibility of a linear motor version. The concept tied in naturally with the production experience, facilities, and marketing capability of two of the corporation's commercial divisions. Through technology transfer, the know-how was made available and an important product group developed.

Similarly, when a comprehensive "clinical" study of the textile industry was required, the man put in charge was an Apollo project graduate who put into practice the systems analysis skills and techniques ideally matched to the task. The study included an evaluation of existing technology in the field, growth trends, production, consumption, market projections, and suggested areas where the company's scientific and technological talents could be most profitably applied. Thanks to the systems approach, the job was done by a fraction of the manpower, in a fraction of the time, and for a fraction of the money it would otherwise have required.

There is great potential for technology transfer in America today. From Apollo itself no more than a microportion of the sociological, managerial, and technical fallout has yet been applied to social and commercial advantage. The benefits to earth transport systems alone, one scientist estimates, will be felt for generations to come.

The social applications
The techniques of technology transfer—which obviously extend beyond technology—have been refined by industry and are being successfully applied in scores of corporations. One major application technique is the transfer of key personnel as illustrated by the textile industry study described.

There is no reason why these concepts could not be applied as well to public institutions as to profit-oriented enterprises. In fact, with the competitive factor less intrusive, information dissemination and exchange should be freer and franker.

What I propose at this point is the establishment of Technology Transfer Arms (TTAs)—interdisciplinary task forces organized to investigate and multiply successful innovation—for every field of social endeavor. Under a TTA network, loan or transfer arrangements might be made in the case of creative social planners and administrators with outstanding achievements so that they can bring their talents and know-how to institutions where they are critically needed. These dedicated reformers—educators, penologists, hospital administrators, law enforcement people, welfare program managers, housing experts, and others—would receive not only the immeasurable gratification of seeing their brainchildren flourish, but the national status and recognition they so richly deserve. In the process—which would include the investigation, evaluation, and dissemination of significant social innovation—society would gain by the multiplication of creative achievement in the same manner multidivisional corporations benefit from their application of technology transfer.

Consumer advocate Ralph Nader, for one, recognizes the importance of spreading the word and repeating the deed when important social contributions are made. He has assigned his Raiders the two-year project of compiling an inventory of "good deeds" in government, labor, and business.

The TTAs would proceed a giant step beyond compilation. Properly organized, administered, and funded, they would coordinate the mammoth task of social restructuring on a nationwide basis and insure maximum application of ideas that have been tested and proved.

8

THE
MEASUREMENT
OF PROGRESS

In business, management by objectives in a very real sense is based on measurement by objectives. Division presidents, general managers, department heads, line supervisors—even the rank and file—are monitored on an ongoing basis. The purpose: to determine how individual and group contributions influence such vital profit factors as sales, production, and quality. It is a difficult and serious undertaking. Programs flourish or are cut depending on the results of measurement; managerial fortunes rise or fall accordingly.

Corporate progress, of course, is easier to measure than social progress. Results are more quantifiable. They are less muddled by internal and external interacting factors, less likely to be distorted by emotional inputs. With individual jobs and stockholder dollars on the line, motivations are clear. A company today has no choice but to measure performance and compare it with established commitments if it is to maintain its competitive standing. Thus the art of measurement has been refined to a relatively high degree of efficiency.

How much of the art is transferable? A great deal, judging from the evidence. For one thing, however important quantification may be in measuring commercial endeavors, we have seen in recent years a growing awareness of the need for broader evaluation as well, with a corresponding development of qualitative measurement techniques.

Techniques have been developed in many modern corporations today to expand evaluation to include such factors as quality of ideas generated, upgrading and development of subordinates, employee morale and risk management. At National Cash Register Company, among others, measurement also involves the weighing of short- versus long-term objectives to guard against undue concentration on current results at the expense of future profitability. And even such imponderables as public relations, advertising, and customer service are now being assessed.

The trend, in short, is toward the development of new and more sophisticated measurement techniques extended to all major areas of operation. The Nestlé Company, for example, employs "return-on-investment analysis" to measure the effectiveness of an individual salesman. It regards each salesman's earnings as an investment, his profit contribution through sales, the return. In this way salesmen can be measured against the same return-on-investment standards applicable to any other kind of performance. One question this answers is: What serves the company's profit goals more effectively—the hiring of additional salesmen or the purchase of more advertising space?

Why not apply this same principle and reasoning to social employees as well? For example, why can't a meaningful measuring rod be created for a prison guard's contribution to his employer's main objective, the rehabilitation of prisoners? If, in making this judgment it turns out that his function is 99 percent custodial, might it not lead to the conclusion that some alternative to continuing guard-force multiplication may be desirable? Would it not be better to segregate the minority of hard-core incorrigibles, for instance, and put more teachers and psychologists to work with the large majority of prisoners who can be rehabilitated, or provide additional occupational and motivational facilities instead of more guns and dogs?

MEASURING SOCIAL PROGRESS

A great many educators, social planners, and government officials these days say they are eager to apply proven measurement techniques to social programs and to develop new techniques for specific situations. In education, for example, does more learning take place when teachers prepare their own lesson programs? Do minority students make greater progress under the tutelage of minority teachers? Does the "open" classroom produce better reading achievement than traditional approaches? Only by developing and applying the proper measurement tools can we get answers to such questions sufficiently revealing and reliable to guide programming and allocation decisions.

Employment, for all our advanced economic data-gathering machinery, is another area filled with confusion and uncertainty. Some years ago the government's Joint Economic Committee pointed out that we need better information about the efforts being made by those classed as "unemployed" to find work, to secure training, to become self-employed. How many are willing to relocate if it means getting work? And who are these people? Are they heads of households, second or third workers in a household, or are they outside a family unit? We need a better fix, social planners argue, on the extent to which the available labor supply is idle or being used each month, including that segment of it interested only in part-time employment, and we need more information about "structural unemployment."

We can't get this data without the measurement tools required to develop it.

Bitter controversy rages today over a variety of proposals designed to revamp America's system of health care insurance. The proposal of Senator Edward M. Kennedy, for one, has drawn a lot of fire. My purpose here is neither to endorse his plan as a panacea nor attack it as a socialized extreme. But he does have a point in his comparison of Social Security, which is enthusiastically accepted by the elderly people it was designed to serve, and private insurance, which is under attack by elderly people, consumer groups, and labor unions. Kennedy notes that Social Security, for all its faults, returns 97 cents out of every dollar to the people who pay into the system, or to their beneficiaries. Under the present medical system, he adds, examples can be pinpointed to show where 93 cents of every health dollar premium is retained by the insurance system and only 7 cents paid out.

Senator Kennedy performs no mystical feats to get his information. Assuming that the data is based on research and not guesswork, isn't it fair to assume further that if he can come up with such a comparison, others can too and that it can be built into the system? And wouldn't it serve the public well to measure all social-resource allocation with objectives—and percentage of investment returned—in mind?

MEASUREMENT AND METHODOLOGY

Socio-Economic Rule 1 as noted in Chapter 2 states: "Tie standards and goals to proven human needs." SEM Rule 2 reads: "Apply funding by results."

Not only is measurement the bridge between goals and results, it is also the vehicle for transporting this nation's social institutions from one side of the river to the other. Constructing the conveyance will require a strong and concentrated effort. Although, as we have pointed out and will continue to point out, some highly effective measurement strategies are in use today, primarily in industry, social applications to date have been severely limited in number. As Drucker states:

> We know . . . that we have to measure results. We also know that with the exception of business, we do not know how to measure results in most organizations.

> It may sound plausible to measure the effectiveness of a mental hospital by how well its beds—a scarce and expensive commodity —are utilized. Yet a study of the mental hospitals of the Veterans Administration brought out that this yardstick leads to mental patients' being kept in the hospital—which, therapeutically, is about the worst thing that can be done to them. Clearly, however, lack of utilization, that is, empty beds, would also not be the right yardstick. How then does one measure whether a mental hospital is doing a good job within the wretched limits of our knowledge of mental diseases?

> And how does one measure whether a university is doing a good job? By the jobs and salaries its students get twenty years after graduation? By that elusive myth, the "reputation" of this or that faculty which, only too often, is nothing but self-praise and good academic propaganda? By the number of Ph.D.s or scientific prizes the alumni have earned? Or by the donations they make to their

alma mater? Each such yardstick bespeaks a value judgment regarding the purpose of the university—and a very narrow one at that. Even if these were the right objectives, such yardsticks measure performance just as dubiously as the count of bed utilization measures performance in the mental hospitals.

Despite the complexities, proven capabilities exist for developing measurement methodology. To evaluate social programs, it is necessary to determine the resources put into a project and then measure the resulting benefit. When it is practical to state the investment and return in dollars, we deal with the same units of measurement employed in business. Take the necessarily simplified example of an education program designed to achieve the "profit" objective of reducing high school dropouts. Here we might assign the quantitative unit of "one" to each student awarded a high school diploma, with decent standards assumed so that achievement is genuine.

Assume further that the quantitative input, a fixed amount of dollars, has been designated to attain this objective. The problem that exists is the perennial one of fund allocation. Alternatives might include the hiring of competent and innovative teachers, the construction of well-equipped facilities, the purchase of audiovisual materials, the purchase of programmed teaching materials, or a combination of several such expenditures.

In most social programs the problem is further complicated by the lack of quantitative inputs and by concern about such intangibles as levels of health, rehabilitation, education, and an improved standard of living. To make assessments in these areas the decision framework—such established techniques as cost-benefit analysis; planning-programming-budgeting system (PPBS); input-output analysis; statistical sampling; extrapolation; and other concepts—are no less valuable. Only the key indicators of the system itself and the cast of characters involved in planning and decision making are changed, with sociologists, psychologists, educators, and penologists supplementing the work of such professionals as economists, accountants, and marketing specialists.

The awareness that it is difficult, at times even impossible, to come up with meaningful standards and monitoring guides should not deter us from establishing a viable base from which to restructure the system. A certain element of instinctive input and human judgment is inevitable in setting up social measurement models. Nor can we borrow intact the economist's technique of examining one variable while assuming that others will remain constant. In socio-economic evaluation, several variables often must be simultaneously manipulated.

ACTION NOW

As I have already noted, we're a crisis-oriented society. We respond with surprising alacrity, but rarely with lasting effectiveness, when an Attica, Watts, or Kent State flares. The human tendency, as we have seen often enough, is to douse that part of the fire that flames the highest instead of setting up procedures to prevent future fires from occurring.

"Action now" doesn't mean—or shouldn't mean—responding on a crash basis when extreme political or public pressures make continued passivity inadvisable. Social remedies devised with pacification in mind almost invariably shortchange the measurement and monitoring aspects of publicly funded programs.

The proven key to effective non-crisis response is planning. So we inevitably return to the simple and elemental basics of good business management.

Crisis management of social institutions is geared to immediate demands made valid in the eyes of administrators by the degree of insistence and decibel level involved. Reasoned Socio-Economic Management is geared to human needs on a long-range basis.

Crisis management assigns top priority to the problem of the moment. SEM gives top priority to human needs over the short and long pull according to their order or urgency. SEM planning is designed to prevent fires from occurring. Fire prevention, as experience bears out, is a primary function of the management information system in the modern corporation.

"No surprises" is the admonition so often heard there. The progression of system development—which begins with needs, winds up with results, and is oiled by measurement—contains significant parallels for business and social endeavor.

In business: The need is implicit—to generate profits.
In society: Human needs must be defined.

In business: Goals and subgoals must be established—sales, production, acquisition, development of manpower and product resources—all directed to the upgrading of profit performance.
In society: Goals and subgoals must similarly be set—"target levels" of acceptable health, education, shelter, employment—all directed to the fulfillment of human needs and, pragmatically, to a reduction of the "client population" causing so great a drain on our cities.

In business: Programs must be designed with the achievement of goals in mind. This involves standard programs—the conventional sales force and its activities, the familiar suggestion system, the standardized programs to reduce scrap and absenteeism and upgrade plant efficiency. It must involve experimental programs as well. Haverhill's, for example, a San Francisco producer of recording equipment, offers executives a complimentary Swiss watch with each purchase of a dictating system. The Insurance Company of North America is running a test in several states to determine the feasibility of direct mail selling to supplement its standard distribution program.
In society: Here too the challenge of social planners and managers is to devise programs to meet goals more quickly and effectively. And in the social sector, even more urgently than in business, the role of imaginative experimentation becomes a critical factor. To achieve the goal of crime reduction, for example, a basketball league for teenagers might be funded and organized in a ghetto area.

So we arrive again at the bridge, at the link between needs and results. Without the proper tools to measure and monitor program achievement, where do we go from here? We don't. We're stymied. Yesterday's answers, of course, were sounded all too clearly: funding by habit and tradition, by rhetoric, by the numbers alone. But, as has been pointed out in the discussion of SEM Rule 2, funding without measurement doesn't work. If a modern corporation financed programs this way, it would fund itself out of business in months. Now, to continue with our parallels:

In business: The modern industrial enterprise, especially where it approaches the size, scope, and complexity of the typical social institution or government agency, bases programming and funding decisions on careful day-to-day, week-to-week, and month-to-month scrutiny of key business indicators. The most obvious indicator relating to the marketing programs referred to above is sales. It's a safe bet that the number of orders Haverhill's receives on the heels of premium advertising in *Fortune* and other publications will be closely monitored. The direct mail experiment of Insurance Company of North America will be similarly assessed. In each instance "target levels" would be set to spell out at precisely what level of return program benefits exceed costs and how these benefits compare with those of alternative programs.

In other areas of business, factors are more difficult to assess and, in many instances, no less important. Employee morale is one example, customer service another. In both these cases, more closely analogous to the social situation, both quantitative and qualitative indicators are applicable. In measuring morale, the number of employee grievances might be significant, along with the incidence of employee turnover and absenteeism. Qualitatively, we might assess morale on the basis of degree of cooperation achieved in meeting departmental objectives, level of work satisfaction as determined by interview and questionnaire, general teamwork and rapport objectively evaluated.

The improvement or decline in quality of service would most obviously be determined by the number of customer complaints. Also significant would be feedback from the field through salesman interview and questionnaire, along with other barometers set up to gauge the corporate image in the marketplace as influenced by the service structure.

In society: Here too, though a greater number of complex factors exist and indicators are harder to monitor, a similar pattern can be followed. Take the basketball league program. There are a variety of indicators that might be established to determine its effectiveness. For example, how is the community responding to the program? One way of finding out is to ask people. Does the program have an impact on the school drop-out rate? Are there fewer gangs roaming the streets and is there, as a result, less crime? What about the attitudes of the teenagers themselves? Is participation significant and enthusiastic? Is team pride replacing the gang pride formerly displayed? We can't attach numbers to all of these indicators. But through careful surveys and investigation we can get answers that, when all indicators are considered in toto, will add up to a more reliable measurement tool than we had in the past.

"FOR THE GOOD OF THE COMMUNITY"

Social programs are presumably designed for the good of the community. But without a reasonably reliable and objectively structured measurement system, the "community" represented is apt to be the faction with the loudest or most articulate voice, the longest switch blades, the biggest vote-getting clout.

We must build into our cost-benefit evaluation system—and this involves merely an introduction of the proper input factors —the machinery to acquaint us with both the plus factors of goal achievement and the undesirable side effects as well. For example, too many noble crusaders recklessly launched could create adverse economic repercussions more serious than the condition we're trying to cure. Endeavoring to restore America's atmosphere and waterways to a state of Ivory Soap purity, the indignation of well-meaning conservationists notwithstanding, would probably require yearly expenditures in excess of the cost of waging the war in Indochina.

As resources expert Hans S. Landsberg points out:

One is apt to view the more disagreeable aspects of modern life, including most prominently those due to the impact of technology, with partiality—often unconsciously. We take for granted that we may drink tap water, eat uncooked fruit or vegetables, and consume milk with no thought of falling victim to a lurking bug. We are reminded of our good fortune only when we travel in parts of the world that require preventive or remedial countermeasures, or when the exceptional case in this country hits the front page. But, customarily, we fail to do much balancing of pluses and minuses. We tend to overlook the fact that the chemical industry produces not only controversial pesticides, but also antibiotics and vaccines; that the automobile whose incomplete fuel combustion fouls the city air does, at the same time, enable us to escape its boundaries and to know the world in a way available a generation or two ago only to the daring or the rich. We are quick to lament the fallen sparrow, but slow to celebrate the fall of Typhoid Mary.

A Brookings Institution study cites outdoor recreation as an illustration of the type of social program where account balancing must be taken into serious consideration. It is not a single homogeneous product, states the report, but a bundle of products. Consequently, we must compare utilities generated by wilderness and by Coney Island; recreation for different age-income groups (young and rich versus old and poor); recreation for different interest groups (swimmers versus birdwatchers); recreation provided free to the users versus that at market or other prices. Each of these comparisons corresponds to actual decisions that must somehow be made.

In addition to dollar figure measurement, the authors propose a physical service unit—"merit-weighted user-days" of outdoor recreation:

The physical service unit is based on the notion that user-days constitute a common denominator for service rendered by government dollars spent on recreation. But a service unit based on this proposition alone would be far too crude to pass the "usefulness test." The unit can be made more productive by introducing a concept of *relative* merit intended to take account of the relative utility engendered by a wide variety of qualitative elements which make the difference between a "poorer" and a "better" recreation program.

If such a measure could be achieved, the decision maker would be in a position to compare the social value of a given number of merit-weighted user days of current outdoor recreation that can be bought for the next million dollars of capital expenditure directly with, for example, the social value of a given number of merit-weighted vehicle-miles that a million dollars would provide. Comparisons could extend to other government programs for which the

end-product measures can meet the "usefulness test" at an acceptable level. The functions of such a measure would be, not to replace,
but to supplement, bring into focus, and provide a frame of reference for other considerations. The measure might also serve to improve the rigor and relevance of the descriptive evaluations and
exhortations that inevitably are fed to legislators.

Measurement and control in a complex monitoring system
are based on hundreds or thousands of conditions and variables.
Adjusting Program A will affect Program B. An allocation for
C will react unfavorably on D. If Program E is funded, Program F may be reduced.

A couple of decades ago, coping with such complexities as
the interacting and side effects of social programs might have
been too confusing a prospect for planners to tackle. This was
before the computer. Today, advanced hardware and software
are developed to deal with virtually unlimited mixes of input
and output. As was proved repeatedly in the computer-aided
formulation of highly ramified space and military decisions, any
desired number of *if* conditions can be programmed into a system and the machine set up to respond accordingly.

Again, attention must be drawn to the Apollo manned space
program. If this nation can produce the incredibly intricate systems of monitoring, measurement, and control required to
shrink the reaches of the universe, it can produce the systems
needed to properly restructure and control health care, education, environmental protection, law enforcement, prisoner rehabilitation, or any other segment of our society.

THE BIG ROADBLOCK

The biggest stumbling block to reform, as I see it, is not our
technological tools or capability, but our human frailties, particularly as they apply to commercial and vested interests. In
every field of social enterprise we inevitably run into a barrage
of conflicting interests and lobbyist pressures.

Take transportation. Group A, representing steel and equipment producers, fights vigorously to expand the number of
trains in use. Group B, representing automotive interests, lauds
the flexibility of buses. Group C, representing environmen-

talists, would ban all buses. Group D, representing the petroleum industry, is in conflict with Groups A and C. Group E, representing large manufacturers of monorail systems, has its own cause to espouse. Group F, representing shopping center interests, is off on a tack of its own.

And so the grinding continues, with merchants and highway contractors, urban planners and architects, homeowners and builders, all getting into the act. The various interests line up to do battle, and not always are the skirmishes honest and honorable. As all too often happens, the faction with the greatest financial backing, the biggest political influence, and the most effective strategies of persuasion—which have been known to range from wining and wenching to outright bribes—is the one to emerge victorious. And almost inevitably, the less ably represented citizen from the community most directly involved with the ultimate social decision is left holding the bag.

What has all of this to do with a scientifically structured system of measurement as advocated under SEM? Quite simply, the objective of such a system would be to weight all decision factors objectively and unemotionally, and then to evaluate them with the public, not the private, good in mind. In short, once such a system was in operation, it could be made to function impartially and free of bias, and this would contribute more than any other factor to lining up social priorities with real human needs.

APPLYING TECHNOLOGY TRANSFER

Technology transfer, the conversion of proven business tactics to established human needs, is applicable on a variety of levels.

Joseph Quick heads a New Jersey-based industrial engineering firm that specializes in reducing indirect labor costs. Working largely with manufacturing companies, he estimates that while some 75 percent of direct labor operations in industry are measured, only about 5 percent of indirect jobs are. About half the personnel in the typical manufacturing company—and a great deal more than half in the typical service firm or nonprofit organization—are indirect workers. It is Quick's contention that 70 percent of indirect tasks are both measurable and controllable. Moreover, when the job is done right, about one-fifth of the tasks are found to be redundant.

However approximate these percentages, such findings have exciting implications for the nonprofit sector. Quick's approach, one long used by time-measurement experts, is to measure the average time needed to perform various kinds of chores. Using these guidelines as a base, he sets standards that he then proceeds to sell to supervisors and employees.

Applying his measurement techniques to industry, Quick already has boosted the clerical productivity of R. L. Polk & Co. by an estimated 20 percent and that of Motorola's product inspectors by a similar amount.

More germane to our discussion, Quick's methods, developed for business, are being applied with marked success to nursing operations in Pittsburgh's Sewickley Valley Hospital. There, considerable savings have been chalked up and the quality of nurse care substantially upgraded, according to the hospital's administrator.

Another industrial engineer, Marvin E. Mundel of Silver Spring, Maryland, has set up a similar program for the Department of the Interior. In this operation the amount of lookup time required for certain types of legal information was logged. On the basis of these guidelines, Mundel formulated standards that, when circulated among the department's lawyers and their fairness ascertained, were wholeheartedly accepted, with future manpower needs reduced as a result.

We see such isolated examples of technology transfer in a handful of nonprofit institutions across the nation. It's a hopeful sign, of course, but a sign nonetheless of the scattered approach.

Particularly hopeful is recent evidence that the federal government is not unmindful of the need for examining new methods of measurement in attempting to achieve the high-priority goal of improved productivity in various segments of its mammoth operation. A special presidential task force is hammering out an index that can measure productivity performance of about 50 percent of the federal government's civilian workforce. The National Aeronautics and Space Administration, the

Office of Management and Budget, and several other federal agencies offer help to local governments that are looking for ways to improve performance in such areas as budgeting, management controls, and law enforcement. The Productivity Commission has a measurement study going in this area too.

The presidential task force is developing broader measures of program effectiveness in terms of public impact, promoting wider use of such business-tested techniques as unit costing, and taking a close look at policies that discourage productivity improvement.

Brian Usilaner, a task force representative from OMB, reports that many capital investment proposals with high rates of return "are not being funded because they compete with program dollars in budget requests and do not affect current operations." This is a pitfall familiar to top business planners. In the profit sector some significant appraisal strategies have been developed that are designed to penalize short-term managerial decisions that defeat long-term objectives.

Government students of measurement are also beginning to criticize various aspects of the "numbers game" in many areas of social endeavor. While crime and arrest statistics are needed, a major function of the police is to prevent crime, and no one has yet devised a way to count prevented crimes. Similarly, says Urban Institute economist Harry Hatry, "tons of garbage collected per man-hour is no guide to how clean the streets are." To improve the productivity measures it is developing, the institute is examining the feasibility of visually inspecting the streets and of regularly surveying citizens regarding the safety of their neighborhoods.

As a raft of publicity already has made clear, nowhere is the need for increased productivity more acute than in our financially vised-in cities. And nowhere is the need more critical for effective measurement techniques that can be used as a base of productivity assessment. Some cities—another hopeful sign—are already turning for assistance to the business sector. Los Angeles has set up a "technical services corporation" that applies systems engineering analysis to urban problems. Memphis and Baton Rouge are using computers to determine the most efficient routings of sanitation trucks.

New York City is perhaps the furthest along in the implementation of sophisticated measurement and, hence, productivity improvement techniques. In the late 1960s, it set up a modified planning-programming-budgeting system (PPBS) to analyze its operations. Among the results were a new fire response policy, the use of "slippery water" in fighting fires, and new air pollution legislation.

In 1971, New York launched a major productivity effort involving virtually every city agency. Scores of projects were defined, ranging from buying portable saws for parks maintenance crews to changing time-off procedures for sanitation men to match workload fluctuations. It is already apparent that some dramatic improvements have been achieved. A study in 1970 revealed that 35 to 38 percent of the Sanitation Department's 4,300 vehicles were out of service at any particular time. By reorganizing and re-equipping its garages, the department cut the figure to around 16 percent. Also, new work methods have boosted the productivity of street maintenance crews, and the city has begun to insert productivity clauses in its contracts with municipal unions. Here is yet another strategy used long and successfully by the business community.

SOCIAL ACTION CREDITS

The advantages of applying Socio-Economic Management principles in general and advanced business measurement techniques in particular to the nonprofit sector have been clearly demonstrated. The problem now is how does one stir settled-in social executives to action?

Unless strong political pressures are brought to bear, even the most exciting innovative idea will stand small chance of wide acceptance. Within the business community no such problem exists. The pressures are inherent. The manager who fails to innovate in response to competitive endeavors will be hit by falling sales and profits. His income will shrink. His job will be in jeopardy.

We need similar incentives and disincentives in the nonprofit sector. There, more often than not, the man responsible for motivation is the elected official on the local, state, or federal level. No one can more effectively provoke a status quo administrator to action than a politician in the district who himself has been aroused. But who will motivate the motivator? And how? The answer is through his personal anxieties. These we all know build up to a climax as election day approaches.

What I propose is a motivational program of social action credits (SACKs) for public office holders. To date, efforts at evaluating public office holders have been concerned with whether they are liberal or conservative or right- or left-wing. That is, just about all attention has been focused on the candidate's political philosophy. But we need another dimension for careful study and evaluation. It is the candidate's interest in and approach to the fulfillment of people-needs, his social accomplishment philosophy. Social action credits would create a high-visibility scorecard on these attitudes and actions on the part of elected officials. Credits would be awarded for achievements clearly in the public interest—productivity gains promoted in nonprofit institutions, including government agencies; measurement strategies successfully installed; technology transfers that result in social profitability. Bad marks, or demerits, would be applied in cases of omissions or actions that clearly constitute a public disservice—perpetuation of obsolete programs or institutions, failure to respond to conditions in need of correction, acting for self-gain at the public's expense.

Who would formulate such judgments? Social action committees (Sack-Coms) would be organized in communities across the nation. Varying from area to area in response to problems, needs and social makeup, these might include distinguished nonpartisan individuals from a variety of disciplines: educators, sociologists, psychologists, urban planners, economists, accountants, representatives of the poor and various ethnic groups, student representatives, consumer advocates, ecologists, and perhaps businessmen with no stake in a particular political party.

Traditionally, rhetoric has played a major role in influencing the electorate. Looks, charm, charisma—they also weigh heavily when voting decisions are made. To a degree this may be justified. Such qualities as appearance, charm, and dynamism certainly are ingredients of leadership. But shouldn't the voter have an independent source of information regarding competitors for office, objectivized to the maximum degree possible?

Usually the candidate blows his own horn, and has a powerful organization behind him to assist in the tooting. Too often, the communications media, at the local level in particular, serve as part of this organization. And too often the befuddled voter is propagandized to the point where, even if he belongs to the painfully small minority that attempts to analyze candidates in some depth, he winds up a victim of the propaganda machine with the most eloquent horn blowers and heaviest funding at its disposal.

The SACK program would, in some measure at least, offset this evil in our present elective system. At election time, individual score sheets would be tallied and extensively aired, publicized, and circularized for all voters to assess. While not the sole criterion for voting decisions, it would at least provide the public with a relatively factual and unbiased tool with which to make its judgments. And most important, since the SACK scorecard would constitute a key instrument of public assessment, public servants presumably would work hard to serve the public, knowing that high marks on the cards would be converted to votes at the polls. And what better incentive than votes for elected officials to light fires under uninspired social planners and administrators?

As Herbert F. DeSimone, former assistant transportation secretary for urban systems, predicts, it may soon become necessary "to consider far-reaching institutional changes within the government structure. The federal role will shift from a detailed review of local projects to measuring performance as a condition of federal funding. It will put the burden of proof at the local level."

The SACK scorecard I propose would help to pinpoint performance effectiveness at the precise spot where impediments to action have historically been fixed, the political domain.

9

THE
SOCIO-ECONOMIC
AUDIT

"Judge of a man by his questions rather than by his answers," Voltaire once wrote.

Success-minded businessmen have come to appreciate that asking the right questions at the right time will pinpoint obstacles to profit performance. Success-minded social managers are discovering the same thing. This is not to say the kind of questions that relate to day-to-day transactions, balances and controls, and office and work efficiency, but rather the kind of questions that concern the broader conceptual aspects of management and performance auditing.

Among both business organizations and nonprofit institutions, the use of the financial audit is widespread. Management audits are also used quite frequently. Now our schools, prisons, and welfare agencies should adopt the socio-economic audit, which is the mechanism for asking the right kinds of performance questions.

The urgency of socio-economic audits was stressed under SEM Rule 4. When billions of dollars of public funds are invested in social programs, the public and its elected representatives deserve a qualitative evaluation of how the funds are applied.

The socio-economic audit is the cornerstone of bull's-eye management, the continuous assessment and reassessment of our social performance: first, to assure that needs have been properly defined, next, that goals have been set in response to these needs, finally, that the goals are being met and on schedule.

Today's responsible corporate manager has become increasingly aware that he cannot afford to take goal fulfillment for granted or leave it to chance. He can't afford to wait for a product to fail, a customer service program to deteriorate, or a market sector to dry up, to evaluate performance. He must keep running tabs on the operation as the indicators require. Nor will he settle for performance evaluation that deals with superficial factors alone. His job is to get to the roots of decisions and the motivations behind them, and he knows it. If goals are misconstrued or if they stray off target, he wants to know why. And if he's a knowledgeable executive, he won't accept easy reassurances or glib explanations.

Historically, in the social sector program, action response has been stronger to symptoms than to studied human needs. In an explosive environment something is always done. More police are provided, more money is pumped in, more beds are made available, more guards are hired, more handouts are doled out. But at best crash action produces no more than temporary solutions, if indeed "solutions" is the word at all.

The socio-economic audit, on the other hand, properly designed and built into the system, deals with underlying causes, managerial frailties, and human motivations. It goes to the root of problems, seeking to determine why men perform as they do and what can be done to make them perform better. It thus prevents crises from erupting.

In both the profit and nonprofit sectors, where improvement is sought, the traditional preoccupation has been with efficiency. There's nothing wrong with this. Program dollars always were in short supply and always will be. Routing waste, reducing costs. and streamlining methods and procedures constitute a vital part of any operation. But not the only part—nor even the most important part.

Before determining that the job is done right, it's essential to determine that the right job is done. And, further, that the right need has been focused on and that the right goal is being met. This is the role of the socio-economic audit in the broad-based SEM plan. The focus is on real human needs, on opportunities and deterrents. The technical-mechanical means of implementation are secondary.

Are the needs being met? That's the basic question. Are youngsters being made employable? Prison inmates rehabilitated? Welfare recipients being made self-sufficient? Are patients getting the quality of health care they require? Are students being educated to function more effectively in society? What kinds of standards are we setting and how well are we applying them?

The perfect poverty program, as has been mentioned, would wind up without any clients to serve. But the client population will not decline as a result of food, clothing, or shelter giveaways, important as they may be. The underlying goal must be to eliminate poverty itself by making welfare recipients employable and employed.

The prison population will not decline because society provides more cells and guards for the growing number of inmates. That's where the socio-economic audit comes in. It doesn't address itself to "How many?" but to "How to?": how to reduce crime by transforming criminals into self-respecting and self-supporting citizens, how to motivate them in such a way as to replace hostility with constructive resolution, how to gear them psychologically to work within, not against, society, how to train them effectively for jobs in the community, how to insure that jobs will be available when they are released.

If a correctional institution is to teach the wrongdoer how to live in society, why don't we tear down the prison walls and set up a prison city on two or three hundred acres in the great unused land areas throughout our nation? In such a city the prisoners could be permitted to elect their own mayor, own city council, own police. They would build their own industries, sell their products to the outside, and grow their own food. Appropriate surveillance could be maintained by guard—counselors who would oversee the general functioning of the city in an ex-officio capacity. The prison city itself may or may not be fenced. People in prisons have all sorts of training and capabilities. Why not put them to work in an environment similar to the society to which we want them to return?

We have some examples of where this has been effective.

The whole concept of Boys Town in Nebraska is based on boys getting together in a community of their own, with tremendous success.

Australia was a penal colony in the eighteenth century. The city of Sydney, which now has a population of three million, was built by lawbreakers. The city was designed by an architect who was a Prisoner of Mother England (POME) there. The roads and tunnels were built by the prisoners working as normal human beings in an environment that needed their creative talents.

It is to goals of this type that the socio-economic audit would be addressed. It deals with human needs where the needs occur. Formulating and funding social programs on a remote-control basis rarely serve clients in the best possible way; too often the hungry diabetic winds up with a meal of sweets.

Ultimately, as is historically the case, it will be public need and public demand that will establish the socio-economic audit as an essential and acknowledged strategy for survival and social restructuring. Already the pressures for increased and more effective visibility are being felt from all quarters of the public sector. Hence the inevitability of the socio-economic audit, itself an inevitable prelude to improved visibility. Senator Walter F. Mondale has written publicly and stated to me personally that he believes the absence of a national public forum has been one of the greatest weaknesses of our social effort. He is convinced that the indications of trouble in our cities were present long before Watts exploded, but there was no national forum where public attention could be given them. There was no national debate on the cities because there was no public national system to gather the information, analyze it, and confront the national conscience with the issues. As a result, for a number of summers we have faced with fear and bewilderment what we should have been facing with reason and social commitment.

THE NEED FOR SOCIO-ECONOMIC AUDITS

Here are some situations and case histories that show how urgent is the need for performance audits.

The charge. New York City's Addiction Services Agency, funded by consumer taxes, has never provided the data by which objective observers could reliably assess the value of its various programs.

The source. New York City Council President Sanford Garelik.

The urgency. Millions of dollars annually have been earmarked during recent years for programs designed to control drug addiction and reduce the crime that results from it. The problem, however, appears to be growing rather than abating. Is it not possible that some of the programs, well meant or not, are something short of effective? When Garelik refused to approve a group of drug-program proposals before the New York City Board of Estimate in the spring of 1972, demanding instead reasonable assurances that tax funds previously spent for this purpose had achieved some demonstrable results, he was doing something that members of the board could well do more often, according to a *New York Times* editorial: demand accountability, insist on performance.

"Careful program audits and independent evaluations are needed throughout the broad spectrum of municipal services," the editorial continues, "but nowhere more than in the fuzzy realm of anti-addiction efforts. This is at best a confused area, beset by rival claims of practitioners of competing treatments."

The charge. Federal and state legislators have been shortsighted and remiss in making financial appropriations for the improvement of our much besieged and maligned judicial system.

The source. Judge Irving R. Kaufman of the U.S. Court of Appeals.

The urgency. Kaufman quotes Chief Justice Warren Burger's observation that the entire cost of the federal judicial system in 1971 amounted to approximately $128 million, or two-thirds the price of a single C-5A airplane. He further points out that from 1965 to 1967, out of $20.6 million allotted to aid state and local governments under the Law Enforcement Assistance Program, about one-quarter of 1 per cent, or $50,000, trickled into court administration.

According to Judge Kaufman, the system is not taking into

proper consideration the surging volume of criminal filings and the mushrooming workload that have hit the courts in recent years. "The total number of such filings," he notes, "exceeded two and one-half times the figure of a decade ago. In the federal courts of appeals, the volume of cases filed has tripled in that same brief span."

The growing backlog of pending cases in America's major urban centers has received the persistent attention of the nation's press. Thousands of individuals sit waiting in cells for months for their cases to come up. Large numbers of criminals are not prosecuted—many are deliberately not even apprehended—as a result of the inability of the machinery to grind quickly enough. Whatever the ultimate solution, surely this underscores the urgency of the situation.

The degree to which increased funding alone might help solve the program—and the actions and changes that should accompany the funding—are matters to be determined by performance auditors knowledgeable in this area. To date, except for a handful of isolated instances, such audits have not been undertaken nor such determinations made.

However valid Kaufman's charge, his point appears extremely well-taken when he states: "Other professions—medicine and teaching come quickly to mind—have discovered that applying modern management techniques and employing paraprofessionals or technicians wherever possible, can bring real gains in improving services."

The rate of progress in the "other professions" is, I suspect, less impressive than the good judge imagines. It is, however, notable and encouraging in some areas. Surely one "modern management technique," the socio-economic audit, would serve advantageously in the long-neglected judiciary and in other social institutions as well.

The charge. "More and more subways are being planned on the assumption of what people want without any data to support it."

The source. Environmental psychologist Harold M. Proshansky, dean of the graduate center of the City University of New York.

The urgency. Proshansky, who rides the New York City subways along with two and a half million other straphangers, keeps a diary of his underground experiences. Over the years, he states, he has been "crushed, insulted, frozen, fried, vomited on, and—of course—delayed." Nobody seems to consider what constitutes a rider's comfort, he claims, or whether there should be separate cars for the elderly, for short journeys, or for other special needs.

With the cooperation of the Metropolitan Transportation Authority, a team of environmental psychologists studied a dozen New York subway stations. The researchers counted people going up and down stairs, followed them to see where they stood on the platforms, and tried to determine why they clumped together in some places and stood far apart in others. Like most of the center's studies, this one was designed to identify the effects on human behavior of the actions and programs paid for out of public moneys. The psychologists also propose a variety of changes in existing subway methods and facilities to observe the resulting reactions of people.

Clearly, more research, analysis, and experimentation of this kind are needed in all our social institutions and services. Until needs are adequately determined, resources will continue to be allocated on a hit-or-miss basis. Goals will either be lacking or haphazardly established. The monitoring of performance and progress will be correspondingly ineffective.

The charge. "The solution to a great many of America's social problems, including education, is known in foreign countries. When will American educators find out about them? . . . Most Americans are abysmally ignorant of education in other countries. This has led to parochialism so severe as to be laughable."

The source. Dr. Daniel E. Griffiths, head of New York University's school of education.

The urgency. What Griffiths advocates is yet another kind of technology transfer, this time from abroad. While most of the world studies American education, he points out, scant notice is paid by educators at home to foreign systems and innovations. For example, we keep building bigger and bigger schools, especially high schools, some having 7,000 or more students. And we continue to fund by the numbers as well. But the schools are not cheaper, Griffiths claims. Student achievement is not proportionate to tax outlay. You get a bigger program, but you do not get better education. One of the fundamental aims of education is to make better human beings. The bigger the school, he believes, the less chance you have.

"The English," Griffiths points out, "never want a high school bigger than 1,200 for grades seven through thirteen, and they keep elementary schools between 200 and 400 pupils. The so-called open classroom comes about because they have small schools.

"They have a single salary scale for the whole country, with a cost-of-living supplement for London. There is one collective bargaining each year between the National Union of Teachers and the British government. One salary scale is not feasible in this country, but we could do it by counties or even by states."

We can learn a great deal from foreign systems about other social services and institutions as well, the educator contends: "Public transportation in most of the larger cities is better than here, so many people use it. Some areas in this country, like Detroit, have no public transportation at all. . . .

"The Germans have developed an incinerator that burns garbage and provides fuel for the creation of energy and heat. We have done nothing about that solution to our power and pollution problems.

"London," he adds, "has largely solved the problem of air pollution on the city by banning the burning of any kind of material. Not even the home fireplace may be used. London has gone to electric power and has been able to eliminate the killer fogs such as those of the 1950s that brought death to 4,000. Do we have to go through that," Griffiths asks, "to get control of pollution?"

Perhaps we could learn something as well from the city of Toronto. Such common urban crimes as muggings and burglaries are rare there. People walk the streets at night without fear. The subways are clean and unpoliced. Slums are scarce. The middle classes aren't fleeing the city, and it is growing and prospering. They must be doing something right, and it could well serve as an example to us.

A comprehensive system of socio-economic audits would

evaluate U.S. social goals and achievements in the light of alternative systems and concepts, not only in this country but all over the world.

The charge. Millions of dollars wasted and widespread under-utilization of employee time as a result of New York City job policies.

The source. A New York State audit conducted by State Controller Arthur Levitt and his staff.

The urgency. In assessing a report of this type, one must take into consideration the political implications and long-standing feud between the city and the state. On the other hand, the assertions made can't be airily dismissed: The productivity of city water meter readers is less than half that of workers doing similar jobs in private industry, building inspectors do not work at least a third of their time, welfare employees assigned to check on client eligibility waste about two-thirds of their time, the daily work of truck crews is equivalent to a half day's performance.

As was made clear earlier, the socio-economic audit deals primarily with the broader aspects of management policy and performance. This contrasts sharply with the conventional financial audit, whose main concern is budgetary figures and controls, and the standard management audit, which probes the efficiency of methods and procedures. Nevertheless, if accurate, the state controller's charges are not only grave, but also reflect on the quality of management and organizational performance, which should be of key concern to socio-economic auditors.

The report states, for example, that "based on our findings [at the Bureau of Water Register] we estimate that the same level of service could have been provided at a cost of $2.1 million rather than the $4.2 million spent by the city." It makes similar charges of mismanagement and waste in connection with a number of other city departments and agencies. Needless to say, the city would probably have some strong arguments in rebuttal. But the point makes itself. I shall make no attempt here to referee the bout between state and city legislators. Unquestionably both would benefit immeasurably from a program of well-directed performance audits, as would officials and legislators at every level of government.

THE NEED FOR ANALYSIS

Two years after Nelson Rockefeller took office as governor of New York in 1959, he launched a project called the Albany Mall. Its purpose was noble enough: to convert drab and dreary Albany, or a good part of it, into a grandiose model of urban renewal. Massively funded, the mall has since been referred to by *Fortune* writer Eleanore Carruth as "a case study of over-ambitious design and gross mismanagement." Others use even harsher words—Instant Stonehenge, Rocky's Erector Set, Nelson's Folly, and a host of other epithets.

Ms. Carruth reels off just a few of the misappropriations: For three special-purpose structures—a health laboratory, meeting center, and cultural center—$102 million was the original estimate; now it is $272 million, an increase of 167 percent. The cost of marble facing alone has been estimated at $20 million. The health department laboratory is priced at three times the going cost for commercial laboratories. The saucer-shaped meeting center, referred to as "The Egg," is expected to cost three times the preliminary estimate. To make matters worse, serious doubts have been raised regarding the need for the facility.

Without dwelling on the mammoth funding involved, it might be interesting to speculate on the extent of the costs that could have been avoided if the project and departments involved in its planning had been subjected to a program of socio-economic audits. Would the mall have been launched to begin with? How might the project have been modified? Would the purpose have seemed quite as noble had consideration been given to other priorities—poverty, drug addiction, education, prison reform, crime control, health care—awaiting those hundreds of millions? How would that $20 million worth of marble facing have stood up when evaluated from the standpoint of human needs fulfillment against, let us say, a sorely needed health care center?

What would have been the damage to a corporation if actual

project expenditures exceeded estimates by 200 and 300 percent? When a company that desires to remain solvent decides to introduce a major new product, for example, it does not indulge in promiscuous funding at the outset, risking millions on the venture. Except in rare situations, it employs extreme care, testing each step of the way. It researches markets extensively to gauge probable acceptance. Where tests are favorable, it frequently goes into limited production on a pilot basis, making changes in response to customer feedback before committing significant resources to the project.

Social projects also lend themselves to such testing and sampling, experience proves. The technology exists to make soundings and set up studies to ascertain the public desirability of programs and proposals. A number of think-tank, management-consulting, and public-accounting firms are uniquely qualified to make such judgments as a result of proven capabilities in such areas as cost-effectiveness analysis and program budgeting. It would seem that such a route would serve human needs far more advantageously than a reckless plunging into large-scale programs based on inspiration, instinct, or political expediency. And it would seem to me that a well-planned system of socio-economic audits would automatically imply such a route.

Basic to all public school education is the ratio of one teacher to 25 students. This ratio is extremely critical because it determines the number of classrooms, the size of schools, the number of teachers, the number of principals, how the entire educational system is structured. I think we have a right to assume that this ratio is a relatively modern, carefully researched formula for maximum effectiveness. This is not so.

The formula was established over 1,500 years ago and can be found in the Babylonian Talmud. There it states in effect that for every teacher there shall be 25 students. If the number of students exceeds 25 but is not more than 40, the teacher shall have an assistant. If there are more than 40 students, there shall be 2 teachers.

Education is essentially communication. When we recognize the great strides made in communication over the past 1,500 years, as well as the tremendous body of knowledge that has accumulated during that same period, many intelligent persons must wonder why we have stayed with this antiquated concept. To the best of my knowledge, the answer is only inertia, and blindly following tradition. To my knowledge no research has ever established that the 1-to-25 ratio is the most effective way for education in the twentieth century. Yet we continue building schools, hiring teachers, spending billions of dollars on the basis of this outmoded approach to education.

A firmly entrenched good management policy in industry is to constantly research and reexamine the way things are being done, always with the view toward improving the overall effectiveness of an organization. Why not apply the same evaluation techniques to education? Appropriate socio-economic audits would point up the absence of adequate attention to research.

SOCIAL REPORTS

Socio-economic audits would inevitably generate social reports. The public sector reports would consist of formal statements for the decision-making and evaluative use of legislators and social planners, and informal releases for the use of the communications media.

Senator Mondale and other leaders of government already have made clear that once public visibility and public forums are created, the momentum of citizen pressures will automatically force and speed reform. Senator Mondale's proposed legislation (Senate bill S.5) calls for the presidential appointment of a Council of Social Advisers. This council would be charged with the responsibility of preparing regular reports for the president on the quality of life in our nation. Increasingly U.S. senators and congressmen are coming to realize that an economic report on our nation no longer suffices to define its condition. A social report is no less important. In my view, the passage of S.5 is long overdue. I also believe that the socio-economic audit would act as a strong visibility aid that would lead to increased public awareness with regard to all levels of governmental and institutional functioning.

The penal system is one example. Controversy long has raged between sociologists and penologists, and indeed within the penal community itself and among lawmakers, regarding the prison's true function in our society. It is a kind of left-handed controversy because no one, regardless of what else he thinks about the question, would oppose the premise that the "correctional" institution must correct. Not even the toughest disciplinarian would dispute that, although his agreement may be of a "Yes but" variety.

The field is overripe for performance audits and evaluative reports based on the findings of behavioral, motivational, and other experts. And I'm not talking about the kind of study that winds up gathering dust in the archives, all 2,376 pages of it. I'm talking about audits and reports that, by virtue of responsibility and authority built into the system, would force both operational and legislative action in line with the findings. I'm talking about controls—from the top on down.

The president of a corporation who failed to respond to customer demand to fill an important gap in the product line would soon see his sales decline and his own job in jeopardy. The funding official who fails to respond to a fact-and-research-based mandate to initiate a system designed to treat prison inmates as human beings instead of as caged animals and so, it is to be hoped, make rehabilitation possible, should have his job placed in jeopardy as well.

In Chapter 3 it was pointed out that historically about 5 percent of the allocated prison dollar goes for correction or rehabilitation while 95 percent is earmarked for "security." About as much true rehabilitation takes place in federal and state penal institutions in this country as in Army stockades. If an inmate winds up rehabilitated it is in spite of the system, not because of it.

It goes without saying that the importance of security in the penal institution cannot be overstressed. Naturally, the hardened recidivist, the incorrigible rapist, murderer, or gunman who is likely to engage in a repeat performance if let out in society, must be closely guarded and closely controlled. But it is at least equally important to recognize that such individuals constitute a very small percentage of the prison population. The majority are screaming for help.

Providing this help is the human thing to do. Pragmatically, it is the only economically feasible course to take. The rehabilitated prisoner winds up paying his way in society. The embittered ex-convict costs society many thousands of dollars a year.

In Utrecht, Holland, a soft-spoken woman director, Professor Anna-Maria Roosenburg, presides over the Van Der Hueven penal institution, in which criminals have become patients. It takes men and women together. The staff ratio is more than one to one. Rooms and wards are unlocked at night. In this "clinic" the patients are scrupulously diagnosed and given individualized treatment. The bulk of the 70 offenders are perpetrators of major crime who have been committed to the care of the government for an indefinite period.

Professor Roosenburg believes that consultation with the patients' families is one of the most important parts of the clinic's work. There are six groups of male patients, one of women. Meals and social activities are taken together. The group arrangements are useful for therapy sessions. There is vocational training and there are written assignments. Instructors run judo classes, "which are very good for people who are all aggression and poor at self-control." The operational word is "people," not "aggression."

Professor Roosenburg has a conviction. People are not asocial because they want to be but because they cannot be social. The so-called professional criminal, the man who chooses deliberately to offend, is a very rare bird—if he exists at all.

Are people who run such an organization out of their minds? Many U.S. prison officials would say so.

On the subject of security, the professor readily concedes that despite the high staff ratio it is relatively easy for a patient to walk out of Utrecht. In sixteen years however, remarkably few have done so. And though two or three sex crimes and some thefts have been committed by escapees (no murder or manslaughter), it would be interesting to speculate on how many crimes have been avoided by the conversion of desperate men into human beings.

It is also interesting to note that crime is lower in Holland than in most other countries and that the incidence of recidivism is so small as to be almost nonexistent. In November 1970 Holland's total prison population, including those on remand, was 3,260, twenty-five of them women. Nor are the bulk of the nation's criminals on the outside instead of in custody. Day or night, it is safe to walk the streets in Holland.

I am not about to suggest that the Roosenburg concept of incarceration will work in America. I frankly have no idea to what extent, if any, it could be applied. But I do know that the American philosophy of 95 percent custody, 5 percent human assistance, is not working out to the advantage of anyone. I know that if penal-institution concepts, policies, and results were audited by skilled analysts we would come up with good reasons as to why it is not working out. And we would produce some innovative recommendations for alternative solutions that, however deficient, could hardly be worse than what we're doing now.

We might even be able to adapt an idea or two of Professor Roosenburg's. Why not? Unless we can prove that the American prison inmate is inherently more evil and less rehabilitatable than his Dutch counterpart.

Slowly—far too slowly—some social planners and administrators are awakening to the realization that when institutional performance is audited, and the audits given teeth by authorized follow-up action, improvement takes place. Plans already have been set up in New York's Nassau County, for example, to analyze the productivity of county employees. The project is being heralded by some federal officials as a possible prototype for government units across the nation. One potential byproduct of the system would be individual recognition and rewards. At present, one spokesman concedes, there is little if any incentive to excel. In government, people traditionally are paid not by merit but by classification.

Commenting on the vast and pervasive social problems that plague New York and other urban centers, a *New York Times* editorial writer notes:

A long time has passed since Jefferson urged "divide the counties into wards" to bring government close to the people. His admonition has merit even in this metropolitan era when government clearly is insufficiently responsive to the people; but many significant reforms could be effected far short of breaking up New York City and trying to fit it back together again like so many pieces to a puzzle. The City Council could be restructured and revitalized;

the office of Deputy Mayor for Administration could be made a meaningful one by conferring on it the power to conduct performance audits.

The same could be said of thousands of other offices, agencies, and institutions from northern Maine to southern California and southern Florida to northernmost Washington.

10

SURVIVAL
SQUADRONS

In the last chapter I discussed socio-economic audits and reports. In this chapter I want to talk about the action follow-up to investigation, analysis, and disclosure.

How often in the past have we witnessed violent eruptions —in Watts, Newark, Attica, Kent State, and elsewhere— followed by well-intentioned studies . . . followed by eloquently inspired promises and pronouncements regarding reform . . . followed by what? By little if any innovation that significantly changed the status quo. Is it any wonder the level of desperation continues to rise?

Programs without teeth never could and never will be able to respond to social problems with any degree of effectiveness. Who can blame the disenchanted ghetto resident who sneers at the social scientist with his voluminous report? Even the best conceived report based on the most effectively conducted socio-economic audit isn't worth the staples used to bind it if it winds up on the shelf.

The task confronting us is to build into our social institutions the implementational methodology that will automatically convert audit recommendations into action. One such technique is the socio-economic council. In view of the urgency involved, it might even be called the "survival squadron."

These activating task forces should be set up at every level of our government and society. In function and composition they would be comparable to the watchdog groups employed by large and sophisticated corporations. In the corporate system, teams of key managers representing a variety of corporate interests and disciplines monitor profit milestones and goals on an ongoing basis.

The purpose is to keep the operation on track. Designated individuals are assigned direct responsibility for the performance of predetermined key indicators. In the corporate enterprise, the fluctuation of these indicators regularly monitored by the task force group is inevitably tied to the funding machinery. If the program remains successfully on target, funds are made available as required for continuation or growth. If the program fails to meet the criterion of profitability, if it outlives its usefulness, if changing circumstances alter assumptions so as to destroy its validity, the funds are cut off.

Socio-economic councils could be set up to monitor social programs and institutions on a continuing basis in precisely the same way. Groups would be composed of interdisciplinary personnel ranging from social scientists and business executives to measurement specialists and institutional experts as the need dictates. A major function of these professionals would be to examine existing programs in education, environment, crime, poverty, drug control, and other areas to determine how well objectives are being met. The focus would be on social profitability—qualitative output and levels of accomplishment —fulfillment of human needs. The socio-economic council's essential task will be to arrive at a determination that SEM principles are being effectively applied in the programs and projects under study.

How do task force groups get organized and into operation? They could be set up in a variety of ways: by team-oriented businessmen looking for a meaningful way to involve themselves in the problems of their community, by citizens alarmed about crime in the streets, by program or agency administrators eager to upgrade institutional effectiveness. And, it is to be hoped, by budgetary authorities, legislators, government executives, and appropriations committees in search of concrete data as a basis for funding decisions.

Organized and activated, the socio-economic council would move into specific areas of social endeavor with all probes working. The data quest would center on two primary questions: How well are objectives being met? What are the program's shortcomings and what must be done to correct them? Task force findings and recommendations would be shared with funding officials, who would evaluate programs and appropriation requests accordingly.

Ideally instituted, a socio-economic council would be activated not when a crisis erupts into violence, but in advance of the boiling point while there is still time to do something about it. Again the business parallel applies. The function of corporate monitoring groups is to insure smooth, surprise-free, uninterrupted profit performance. The function of the social monitoring group would be to insure smooth, surprise-free, uninterrupted social profitability.

PROBLEM CITY TASK FORCE

Take a hypothetical example: Problem City, U.S.A. Crime keeps edging upward, muggings and robberies especially, a source of increasing concern to inhabitants. The elderly in particular are terrorized. Women are afraid to walk the streets alone. Apartments become padlocked prisons at night. Storekeepers are fearful and desperate.

A socio-economic task force group is organized to deal with this specific problem. Getting out into the neighborhood, they conduct an intensive probe or feasibility study. It reveals:

1. Teenage gangs are responsible for most of the muggings and robberies. The age range is 11 to 18 years. Many of the older youths have police records already. When things get too hot in Problem City, the more hardened and seasoned young hoodlums extend operations to other communities.

2. Teenage delinquency is on the rise. Gangs are getting bigger. New gangs are formed from time to time. Most of the mugger and robber recruits are school dropouts.

3. Teachers report characteristics of budding dropouts: unresponsive in class, do not do their homework, get low grades, are truant and frequently in trouble, generally use drugs.

4. No agency exists that is clearly and specifically responsible for dealing with this problem from beginning to end.

5. Psychologists, educators, and sociologists believe there is

no quick solution for present gang members, many of whom are already hardened and have had contacts with the police.

6. The most hopeful starting place to attack the problem is the pre-gang stage, before the potential dropout shrugs away positive values and resigns himself to crime. Here it is possible to stem the flow of new recruits.

After the research is complete, the interdisciplinary socio-economic council evaluates the findings, explores alternatives, and makes the following recommendations:

1. Assisted by teachers and psychologists, identify 20 youngsters who are potential high school dropouts and teenage offenders.

2. Remove them from school now so they will no longer have to attend classes or report to their teachers or other authorities.

3. Under Board of Education auspices and through a dedicated school administrator who enjoys proven rapport with youngsters, bring the 20 youths together. In consultation with them, and with educators, psychologists, and sociologists, pinpoint their major interests. Assume, for example, that they would all like to learn how to take apart, put together, and repair automobiles.

4. Make available to the administrator and this group a vacant building in the area to serve as a laboratory. Bring in a skilled automechanics instructor and devise a program of pay-as-you-learn training for the youngsters. The pay will be based on number of hours spent learning and working in the laboratory.

5. Arrange with service stations and garages in the area to place the trainees as assistant mechanics when they become qualified.

6. As an incentive to employers, arrange to pay each proprietor from 50 percent to 100 percent of the trainee's first year's wages.

7. Project funding would match appropriations already provided to each school for each student. If the high school receives $3,000 per year per student, the funding would total $60,000 (20 × $3,000). Additional financing might come from

money paid for automobile repairs made by advanced student groups. If a funding slack still exists, it could be taken up by city authorities from allocations already made for law enforcement, prevention of teenage delinquency, or special educational projects.

As the project gets under way and becomes a functioning entity, the socio-economic council will monitor its effectiveness through an ongoing program of socio-economic audits.

Who would serve on such a council? Educators, psychologists, criminologists, sociologists, business executives, measurement experts. A variety of disciplines would be needed, the stress being on contribution to objectives directed by program requirements. Disciplines would interact with and complement one another.

The educator would evaluate and report on learning achievement and potential. The psychologist would augment and reinforce the educator's judgment. He would analyze and predict behavioral response and suggest techniques to stimulate cooperative participation. The criminologist would stay alert for signs of antisocial and criminal tendencies. He would help with the task of steering youngsters clear of known criminals and drug pushers. The sociologist would help prepare rehabilitants for a constructive, self-fulfilling role in society.

The business executive, trained to keep projects moving and targets on schedule, would monitor progress, prevent roadblocks from occurring, and help debureaucratize the program. He would tailor motivational incentives to program needs, assist with planning, organization, and goal-setting functions. The measurement expert—accountant—would help devise standards, set up program controls, evaluate milestone achievements against projected results at predetermined periods, design socio-economic audits, and assess levels of accomplishment.

Whether funded as part of an official social agency or as an independently formed citizen group, to be most effective the task force would operate outside the institution itself. By virtue of its continuing program of social audits and social reports, it would serve the dual purpose of gadfly and communications link with the public. Thus it would create the visibility required to produce the social pressures that move legislators, politicians, and administrators to action, and convert well-meant recommendations into positive results.

MULTIPLICATION WITHOUT GROWTH

Massive and growing social and government institutions, like the cities that contain them, must be closely monitored if they are not to add pieces and duplicate effort on an ad hoc basis. The syndrome seems to manifest itself in functions and subfunctions all down the line. The resulting waste costs taxpayers millions, defeats program objectives, and dries up desperately needed funding sources.

Take the simple example of roadway repairs. A piece of Broadway is first repaired by order of a roadwork authority. It is torn up soon after by order of a gas distribution authority. When an order comes through from the electrical supply authority, it is torn up again. Not to be outdone, the water supply authority gets into the act. Traffic is snarled. Residents and merchants of the area suffer annoyance and inconvenience. The noise and dirt level rise. Dollars are drained by the repeated labor costs. The waste is apparent.

Ten years ago, New York City had 253,000 employees with a total payroll of $1.2 billion and an expense budget of $2.4 billion. As of this writing, it has 413,000 employees with a total payroll of $3.4 billion and an expense budget in the range of $9 billion in the present year.

The city's population is just about where it was ten years ago, approximately eight million. During this same period, the number of Board of Education employees rose from 56,000 to 105,000, while the pupil population increased only 15 percent. Other departments, such as police, fire, sanitation, had increases ranging from about 13 to 45 percent. If this is the case in New York City, it is probably the case in most other large cities as well.

Where do we look for solutions? We must go back to the basic principles that govern the operations of businesses. They have to compete; to organize and reorganize constantly in response to change; to install modern systems, equipment, and techniques; to improve their products and services; to streamline their production; to simplify their distribution; and to be efficient in order to survive.

But local governments have gone on operating pretty much along the lines of organization and management that would have characterized a country general store several decades ago. Today the lack of efficiency in local government is undermining the total efficiency of the cities as economic entities—at the very time when they must compete in the fast-changing national and world markets of today and tomorrow.

Apart from the vast financial toll, the greatest danger of all lies in the unchecked deterioration of governmental services and their adverse effect on the national economy as a whole.

If we are to look to modern business principles and techniques for solutions, the corporate-type multidisciplinary task force I recommend is almost automatically implied. I can visualize the benefits of such a body of experts applied to every aspect of social endeavor. Nor am I alone in my urging. Commenting on environmental changes that trigger a sequence of irreversible effects, resources economist Nathaniel Wollman notes:

> We cannot expect [environmental] decisions to be both "correct" and based upon democratic authority unless the electorate is well-informed and aesthetically sensitive. Lacking these qualities but aware of the deficiency, the electorate can proceed with confidence if there is a qualified body to whom it can delegate responsibility. Since all levels of government have environmental problems to solve, there is need for a corresponding hierarchy of environmental boards of experts. These boards should possess the power and authority that is now accorded the military establishment, not only because the penalty of inexpert decisions may be just as disastrous for the human race as the effect of military weapons, but because the ability of most of us to make expert decisions is no greater in the field of ecology, broadly conceived, than in warfare.

As an adjunct and follow-up to Socio-Economic Management we would be well served by an array of socio-economic councils, action-geared task force groups, multidisciplinary survival squadrons—call them what you will—at every level of public enterprise.

SOCIO-ECONOMIC COUNCILS IN ACTION

New York City's criminal courts. "It is my conviction," notes EDC president George Champion, "that if the cities take advantage of the tremendous pool of modern management methods, systems, talent, and techniques available in the business community, there can be a new day in the history of the urban crisis. This statement, I realize, would be merely interesting if it resided in the realm of theory. But today it rests on a developing record of experience and demonstrable fact."

In July 1970, the Economic Development Council formed a ten-man task force to conduct an organization study of the New York City Criminal Court. The team, headed by Metropolitan Life Insurance Co. Vice-President Harold A. Finley, a nationally known business expert and analyst, consisted of executives "on loan." At no cost to state or city taxpayers, it worked nine full months to produce a series of recommendations for fundamental improvements in the organization and operation of the criminal courts.

The study was long overdue. Early probes were revealing: a staggering backlog of cases, with 400,000 new cases produced each year; some cases dropped because witnesses were dead or had memory lapses; hardened criminals walking the streets for months, free on bail because their cases couldn't be scheduled; other thousands languishing in jail awaiting trial; court records a shambles; court business transacted in crowded corridors because offices and waiting rooms were unavailable. The system was no system at all.

Cutting through this maze of inefficiency and confusion, the task force got down to the basics of business and management. It came up with a series of specific action steps to restructure the criminal court network, clarify lines of command, modernize record keeping with an integrated information system, and set up cost controls and performance incentives.

The judiciary itself stood solidly behind the group. At EDC's Fifth Annual Meeting, presiding Justice Harold A. Stevens of the appellate division remarked: "The report, as presented, and later issued to the public, highlighted administrative problems in the Court and offered specific recommendations for improved organization, management, and efficiency. It is magnificent! Many of its recommendations have been implemented; in fact, a restructuring and reorganization of the Criminal Court is well under way. . . . It is a landmark in pointing out to the entire nation how the private and public sectors can work together for the common good and join in seeking reform in the Court."

Most important, the power to implement task force recommendations was provided by the court system itself. A new administrative judge, David Ross, was brought in from the New York Supreme Court and placed in charge of the restructuring. He saw to it personally that recommendations adopted were followed by action.

The results were dramatic. Only ten months after reorganization, the number of backlogged cases was cut 58 percent—from 59,406 to less than 25,000, the first such reduction in 18 years. The number of jailed defendants awaiting trial was slashed in one year from 3,176 to 2,385. "Today," says Ross, "there is no reason why an incarcerated defendant can't have a trial in this court in two weeks if he wants it."

Obviously the key to the problems of our cities lies not in hiring more people and buying more facilities, but in applying businesslike management practices to the people and facilities we have.

Task force linkage. There is, as Franklin A. Lindsay points out, a large area of social enterprise that neither the public agency nor the private corporation can handle effectively. Deficiencies in training, experience, and resources impair efficiency and undermine objectives. A nationwide network of socio-economic councils would help immeasurably. They would serve, first, to pinpoint needs and causes, next, to harness the disciplines required to battle inefficiency, and finally, to bring human and physical resources together into goal-directed movement. To achieve this, notes Lindsay, new action units must be developed.

What kind of units? Public-private hybrids that combine the best attributes of government—funds, political capacity, public accountability—and private enterprise—systems analysis, technology, managerial implementation—in optimum problem-solving combines.

American ingenuity should be able to apply such capabilities to urban, housing, transportation, and other problems. The forerunners and models already exist. One such model is the twin Bedford Stuyvesant Corporations in New York City. It aims at the comprehensive redevelopment of a deteriorating inner city. One of the twins is a restoration corporation. Its directors are community leaders. With a controlling voice in decisions affecting their lives vested in area residents, constructive citizen participation is assured. The other twin is a development and services corporation whose board is drawn from the nation's business and financial leadership. The contribution of the latter, apart from financial guidance, is the application of managerial expertise to the venture.

A similar cooperative undertaking is the New York State Urban Development Corporation. Its purpose is to help renew New York's cities and towns and assist in planning the orderly growth of new urban areas. Five of UDC's nine directors are private citizens appointed by the governor. A business advisory council, working with local advisory committees, makes recommendations on development policies and programs and helps recruit additional business participation and support.

On both the state and local levels these groups combine the energies, skills, and dedication of private and public executives to design and implement "total system" concepts as set up in advanced corporate planning rooms. Areas of operation range from housing and training to the expansion and revitalization of industry.

Admittedly, these are large and ambitious ventures. But as evidence bears out, public-private teamwork serves equally well on more modest endeavors. Within or independently of state and city agencies, concentrated efforts could be organized and task forces set up—as was done for the criminal court study— to deal with local or neighborhood problems.

Brownstone revival. One proven way to stem neighborhood deterioration and so prevent slums from forming is building restoration. In 1968 the Economic Development Council, sensitive to the symptoms of area decline, discovered an exciting "hidden asset" throughout all of New York City. In a score of communities thousands of fine old townhouses—"brownstones" dating back to the nineteenth century—were identified and listed. Many of them had fallen into disrepair through the years, but most were structurally sound and worthy of rehabilitation.

Using the tested task force approach, EDC formed the Brownstone Revival Committee to encourage New Yorkers to buy and rehabilitate these stately structures into modern family dwellings. "Brownstoners," as the committee members are known, are drawn largely from executive and professional ranks. They have become, among other things, a clearinghouse for information. The committee issues a bimonthly newsletter with financing, restoration, and other data. In 1968, it published a "Home-Buyer's Guide to New York City Brownstone Neighborhoods." It also conducts surveys and seminars, contacts neighborhood associations, and maintains liaison with major banks, utilities, and insurance companies.

Needs-oriented, following the goal-directed techniques of corporate committees set up to fulfill specified accomplishments by a given date, the organization takes whatever steps are necessary—from investigation to field action—to get the job done. As a result, whole neighborhoods have been redeemed —some on an integrated basis. The city's tax revenues have been substantially increased. Best of all, the city's population "mix" is being improved by the infusion of good young citizens and their families.

THE ACTIVATING THRUST

If spirit and dedication were measurable and a survey could be taken, the revelation that social scientists and planners more often than not are an exemplary group among American professionals would come as no surprise to me. Unfortunately, however, it takes more than an inspired yearning for reform to bring it about. It takes the hardnosed, pragmatic approach as well.

That's why the so-called multidisciplinary approach to social restructuring is so important. Because this vital ingredient was missing from a majority of social endeavors in the past, innumerable failures resulted. As HEW's William Gorham, testifying in 1967 before a Senate subcommittee probing government operations, stated: ". . . it is probably true that a majority of social scientists agree that they should aspire to be 'scientific.' " This means, he explained, that they strive for detachment rather than commitment and that they conceive their task to be that of studying the consistency of means and ends, rather than of specifying what ends or values should be sought. According to this conception, the social scientist engages in positivistic studies of the way given social, political, and economic systems function, and asserts that on normative questions—those that ask what we ought to do in some moral sense—he has, as a social scientist, no *professional* opinion.

He went on to point out that the social scientist, trained to avoid sensationalism and to adhere rigidly to "scientific principles," is inclined toward jargon and complexity rather than fire and spirit. At the same time the fact that the social scientist researcher earns his daily bread by working at the frontier of knowledge gives him a lively sense of the limits of our knowledge. He is therefore prone to plead for further research before committing himself.

Mancur Olson, Jr., also of HEW at the time, echoed this view. "We should hope for a great deal of disciplinary overlap," he says, "so that every problem that might benefit will, if the available resources permit, get the benefit of attention of scholars with different attitudes and methodologies."

As Gorham pointed out at the hearings, other witnesses before the subcommittee recommended that members of the humanities, representatives of the disadvantaged, elder statesmen, clergymen, civil rights activists, and businessmen should be included on action and study groups. He adds: "Any body that is designed to pass judgment on the performance of particular departments, and help decide which should be expanded and which should be contracted will by definition have an impact on the budgetary process."

This virtually demands the inclusion of budgeting and allocations experts. Gorham's testimony related to the makeup of a

Presidential council of social advisers. He expressed doubt that such a body could operate effectively without the proper complement of overlapping disciplines. His point, I believe, is valid for socio-economic councils on any level.

The businessman is accustomed to setting deadlines and seeing that they are met on schedule. The community representative is pressured by his "constituency" to produce results. The professional in the field deals with problems and their consequences on a day-to-day basis. An abundance of evidence proves that when such men and women join forces with dedicated social scientists, planners, and administrators, not only do problems get analyzed, the job gets done as well.

"MASSIVE COLLABORATION"

There is no single solution to any of this nation's complex social problems. But I strongly believe with David Rockefeller that one of our pressing needs "is for more massive collaboration by groups of corporations in diverse fields to tackle some of those major problems that surpass the resources of a single company. Businesses must learn to create consortiums to achieve social objectives so as to surmount their fears of inadequate effort, unsophisticated effort, and effort exploited by free riders."

Ideally, such efforts could be put to most profitable use if expended jointly and cooperatively with existing social institutions and agencies. The accomplishment and waste-reduction potential of such teamwork would be exciting.

A recent CBS-TV special report depicted the plight of a widowed black woman in Harlem. With missionary zeal she provided food, shelter, and an abundance of love for the abandoned children of drug addicts, alcoholics, and other society dropouts. With the assistance of two or three part-time helpers, she was caring for 26 youngsters, some of whom were infants. All were impossibly crammed into a meager five-room apartment.

Understandably, this remarkable woman's selfless work attracted the attention of the Office of Economic Opportunity. Funding of $400,000 was granted for an "institute" to be housed in an ample building in the neighborhood where the "mother of 26," with the aid of hired assistants, could develop and expand her activity. In charge of the project? The widowed black woman and her helpers.

What could she conceivably know about setting up plans, formulating goals, establishing standards, applying funding by results? Her chief "disciplines" in life are compassion and love. Predictably, in her dealings with architects, lawyers, and contractors—while simultaneously attempting to care for her charges—she found herself bewildered, and the project became hopelessly snarled. At this writing, the architect is up in arms, the contractor has walked off the job, and the lawyer has no solution. As a result OEO funding has been stopped and the program shut down, temporarily at least. It is to be hoped that the exposure provided by CBS will get things going again before too long.

The victims? Dozens of homeless children whose lives might be salvaged if the job were done right. Where was the task force of experts—the socio-economic council—so obviously and desperately required to tackle this relatively simple project and bring it to fruition?

There's little question in my judgment that if a task-force–oriented organization had been on the scene, the outcome would have been different. But there are too few such groups in our society today, and their time and their resources are limited.

Why not, then, a central clearinghouse of socio-economic councils or task-force–building entities to which such cases could be referred? Set up in major urban areas, they could eliminate a tremendous amount of waste and frustration. Had such a group existed at the time of that $400,000 funding, how much more sense it would have made for OEO to designate this as the supervising arm of the child care "institute."

NATIONWIDE NETWORK

Socio-economic councils, flexible in organization and format, could be set up to fulfill an infinite variety of objectives.

An area where public-private cooperative ventures might be

applied beneficially is in the development of entirely new towns, satellite cities, and new sections within existing cities to accommodate the millions more Americans who will live in this country by the year 2000. Although the bulk of the new growth will come through expansion of existing communities, a significant supplement could come through newly created towns and cities. About a dozen of these new towns are now being built, such as Reston, Virginia, and Columbia, Maryland, but the need is for hundreds more to provide adequately for our additional population without increasing even more alarmingly the crises in our cities.

In the planning and construction of new towns, every conceivable social and management discipline could be put to profitable use. The same case might be made for a variety of endeavors ranging from transportation and health care to education and crime control. The need will be to apply our human and capital resources not singularly, to problems as they arise, but cooperatively, from the early planning stages, through the fulfillment of predetermined milestones, to the achievement of jointly agreed-upon goals.

FRAMEWORK FOR THE FUTURE

Of the scattering of U.S. organizations, private and public, established to apply the resources of business to America's social problems, the Economic Development Council's work is particularly noteworthy. Despite some inevitable failures and disappointments, it has done as well as any group I know in operating effectively and fulfilling stated objectives.

The success EDC has enjoyed to date stems from an innovative combination of six important principles:

1. The direct application of specialized executive talent by corporations willing to contribute the services of outstanding personnel on a full-time, "on loan" basis. Only men of the highest qualifications are chosen. They work in much the same spirit as did the dollar-a-year men in wartime Washington.

2. Executives assistance is provided only at the specific request of the agency heads involved—and then only when a

clear-cut statement of objectives, plan of action, and implementation is agreed upon in advance.

3. EDC deals with all public officials on a completely non-partisan basis. Publication of findings is withheld throughout the period of the study. The report and recommendations are stated in wholly impersonal and factual terms.

4. The full cooperation of agency heads and staff is assured by the constructive approach and complete objectivity of the task forces. They seek simply to be helpful and they have no axe to grind.

5. The emphasis on implementation distinguishes the EDC's approach from other such studies. Prior agreement that the task forces will remain on the job during the implementation is not only unique but vital.

6. Documentation is an essential step in the total process. It serves as the link between the pilot application of the programs in New York and the potentially nationwide adaptation of these principles in city after city and agency after agency.

Obviously, the manpower and methodology exist. We have only to use them.

11

THE CORPORATE
SOCIAL AUDIT

We have been pelted of late by a hailstorm of corporate pronouncements on social involvement such as has never before been witnessed.

"We pledge," says one president, "to devote every human and financial resource at our disposal to the job of cleaning up America and making it a better place to live in."

"We hold social responsibility," says another, "to be our No. 1 corporate objective in the years ahead."

A third proclaims that "the company which fails to contribute to the betterment of the community will surely perish."

Almost daily we read in the press the pronouncements of chief executives who equate such causes as the hiring of minority groups, the training of disadvantaged persons, and environmental cleanup with good business management.

In some cases, corporate actions add bite to corporate pronouncements, and in progressive organizations, as the sampling in the previous chapter makes clear, a genuine effort to redress wrongs and turn society around is being made. Also, the evidence of real sacrifices by honestly concerned individuals and corporations is on the rise.

But that's one side of the picture only, and, quantitatively at least, real sacrifices are in the minority. Too many corporate chiefs have not been heard from to date. With others, lip service is the principal contribution. They confirm the need for swift and drastic change and proclaim the importance of corrective action geared to social improvement. But when dollar cost is involved, their conviction seems to falter. When it comes down to the hard business decision of whether or not to participate in areas of social responsibility, ideals sometimes are abandoned in favor of the short-term profit lure.

The men and women of America who hold the top corporate positions know that you cannot run on a collision course with history without ultimately crashing. But the temptation is great to brush social action aside, to yield to the pressures of here and now. Somehow, the reasoning goes, the long-range situation will take care of itself. It always has in the past.

So the buck is passed and the expenditure dollar is protected, at least for the present. Such reasoning makes sense—up to a point. It's realistic and practical. In fact, often the worst corporate abusers of the environment and humanity manage to look the best on their profit and loss statements, at least in the short run.

Sophisticated analysts have long been aware that those managements that neglect plant facilities, cut back training and development investment, and retrench on long-term promotion and advertising will show a higher earnings performance than justified. Yet in time, false economy takes its toll. The sweets of today turn bitter. But that comes later. Similarly, a company can show good operating profits by dumping poisonous production wastes into the atmosphere or waterways and ignoring the consequences, or by grinding out salable products that jeopardize people's health.

To date, corporate accountability for socially responsible action has been largely nonexistent. Our present system of business reporting does not indict management for scarring the land with strip mining or blotting the beaches with oil slicks. Nor does it credit management for training efforts that convert semiliterate welfare recipients into self-supporting technicians, or the donation of talented executives to community causes.

Herein lies the challenge, and all the signs point to a positive response. Because of the increasing exposure of business to the various facets of society, the traditional measurement of profitability and growth as reflected both in the profit and loss statement and the balance sheet is no longer adequate. Business management today is functioning in a new environment. Increasingly, it will be forced to assume its equitable share of social responsibility.

The minority of companies that are putting dollars and manpower on the line for the benefit of society are beginning to realize it is unfair to be penalized on their earnings statements for responsible citizenship. It is unfair to mar the corporation's financial image because of extra money paid out to hire and train the hard-core unemployed, because of executive assistance to ghetto entrepreneurs, or because of purchasing costly equipment to neutralize poisonous wastes before emptying them into our streams. This state of affairs cannot continue. A means must be found for properly reflecting all aspects of managerial endeavor, positive and negative. We must build into our system a chain of incentives and disincentives for rewarding social responsibility and penalizing social irresponsibility.

PUBLIC VISIBILITY IS THE KEY

Public visibility, the tool to accomplish this end, has long been at hand. But perhaps it has been too obvious. Public visibility, properly implemented, will make it unprofitable for corporations to avoid carrying out their responsibility to society. Its leverage potential is great.

The evidence of this potential has multiplied in recent years. Public visibility during 1972, for example, and the concern that it generated, caused school bussing to emerge as a major campaign issue. Public visibility in our time, and the nationwide heat it produced over an unpopular war, caused one president to pull out of the political arena and another to wind down hostilities and withdraw troops from Asia on a wholesale basis.

Public visibility today, and the action it produces, already is in the process of creating safer cars and highways, influencing the detergent buying habits of consumers, sweeping candidates into office and out, and changing investor habits and attitudes. It's also playing a vital role in the promotion of new legislation to make advertising more truthful, lending less deceptive, and insurance rules more equitable.

It is no secret to John Citizen, to the politician he elects, or to the head of the company that employs him, that when you stir up public concern, remarkable things can be made to happen. Remarkable, even to the point of genuinely inspiring social responsibility.

Much has been said about the need for better measurement and follow-up accountability in social programs, but opinions as to how to do it vary greatly. The biggest mistake we could make at this juncture, I believe, would be to try to design techniques that would fully satisfy all dimensions.

It may be years before we can invent and use social measurement with the confidence and relative accuracy with which we use fiscal and economic measurement in business and government. But we have sufficient social standards and data on hand to get off to a start. I might venture to add that considering the softness and misuse of many fiscal and economic measurement tools in operation today, social measurement tools, despite their limitations, could be made at least as effective.

What we can do at once is to borrow from economics and finance what we know of the system that works and apply it to the corporate fulfillment of social responsibility. This is what socio-economic measurement—and the kind of reporting that creates public visibility—is all about.

There are many factors in our favor. Dollars relating to social costs incurred by a company are clearly determinable. That a statement which outlines these costs may be incomplete is no reason to put off its preparation. What we need is a launching point.

Here I present a suggested beginning. The format is simple. Its title: The Socio-Economic Operating Statement (SEOS).

The SEOS would be prepared periodically, along with the corporation's balance sheet and profit and loss statement. It would tabulate those expenditures made voluntarily with social improvement in mind. Employee welfare (other than the mandatory costs of doing business), product safety, and environmental protection are typical items that might be included. Expenditures required by law or union contract would not apply.

Negative, or "detriment," items would be detailed to offset these *pro bono publico* expenditures. These would include programs to improve employee welfare, product safety, environmental protection, and so forth, which a progressive, modern, socially conscious management would be expected to undertake but which this management decides to ignore or postpone.

The SEOS statements themselves would be prepared by a small interdisciplinary team with predetermined accounting principles and controls adhered to. Team members would include an accountant, a seasoned business executive, a sociologist, a public health administrator, an economist, and other professionals whose particular expertise might apply to a given industry or circumstance. Although SEOS statements ordinarily would be prepared internally, they would be audited by an outside, similarly qualified interdisciplinary group.

The SEOS purpose is as simple as it is clear: to report to management and to hold up to public scrutiny what a corporation has done for society on the one hand, and what it has failed to do on the other.

Obviously, the task of developing the SEOS and determining which costs should be included and which left out would not always be clear-cut. Companies want to look good and will fight for their image. Distinctions would have to be made between mandatory and voluntary costs. Definitions of what truly constitutes the public good and what constitutes the corporate good would have to be spelled out. Differences of opinion would be inevitable and would be dealt with in stride, just as differences over the content of financial accounting statements have been dealt with for decades. As any financial executive knows, the records are loaded with rules of accounting and reporting, contested, altered, and refined on an ongoing basis with the assistance of the accounting profession, the SEC, and other regulatory agencies.

Differences or not, the P&L statement presently fulfills its function, the balance sheet likewise. What I am suggesting is that in the battle for survival we are waging today, the function of SEOS is no less urgent. There is no reason why it could not be developed and honed in precisely the same manner as have the more mundane statements it would accompany.

RESOLVING DIFFERENCES

Ultimate SEOS guidelines could be worked out by a duly authorized board or commission set up for the purpose. Similarly, arguments would be heard and resolved. Detriment items or negative charges would be brought to management's attention through the appropriate machinery. Management would thus be given ample opportunity to respond.

Determinations may be largely subjective at times. This should not discourage the implementation of SEOS. Accounting treatment and financial analysis, research and development items, work in process inventories, allowances for bad debts, depreciation charges, price-earnings ratios, and the like are also largely subjective.

Public visibility of the SEOS would act as a strong motivator for business executives, and as a healthy corporate equalizer as well—giving the socially responsive company as well as the less responsive its due. One may easily predict some thoughtful reflection in corporate suites where "Let George do it" attitudes traditionally prevail, if it is now apparent that if George does it and you don't, he will be publicly recognized and you will not.

To take public visibility a step further: On an annual basis, for example, we might expect *Fortune's* "Annual Survey of Corporate Responsibility." This, as would reports in *Business Week* and the *Wall Street Journal*, would summarize a corporation's net social contribution—or deficit—and present it in print for all to see. Nor is there any reason to suspect that *Newsweek, Time, The New York Times,* and other general publications would not follow suit. The press would also engage in the game of drawing corporate comparisons on a national, regional, and industry basis.

THE SOCIO-ECONOMIC DOLLAR

The dollar amounts included in an SEOS would be a combination of what businessmen traditionally categorize as capital and expense expenditures. For reference convenience, the totals might be designated as being expressible in socio-economic dollars (SE$).

The socio-economic dollar would be a unit of measurement used to identify all socially beneficial expenditures made voluntarily by a corporation. The full cost of a permanent installation of a pollution-control device, for example, would be reflected in the SEOS statement in the year the cost was incurred.

The annual operating cost of a hard-core minority group training program would be treated in the same manner.

A network of rules and regulations governing permissible SEOS items and procedures would be established and refined on an ongoing basis. To illustrate:

1. If a socially beneficial action is required by enforceable law, it would not qualify for SEOS inclusion.

2. If a socially beneficial action is required by law, but is ignored, the cost of such an item would be charged as a "detriment" for the year. The same treatment would be given to an item if postponed, even with government approval.

3. A pro-rata portion of salaries and related expenses of personnel spending time in socially beneficial activities or with social organizations would be included.

4. Cash and product contributions to social institutions and social causes would be designated under "improvements."

5. The cost of setting up facilities for the general good of employees or the public—without union or government requirement—would be includable.

6. Expenditures made voluntarily for the installation of safety devices on the premises or innovations that reduce product hazards would be includable if not required by contract or law.

7. Neglecting to install safety devices that are available at reasonable cost would be a "detriment."

8. Community improvements, such as the cost of voluntarily building a playground or nursery school for employees or area residents, would reflect positively on the statement. Operating costs of the facility on a year-to-year basis would also be includable.

9. The cost of relandscaping strip mining sites or other environmental eyesores, if not required by law, would be displayed as an "improvement" on the SEOS exhibit.

10. The "esthetic" costs of designing and installing beauty into business facilities for the purpose of enhancing the environment, as opposed to the purely functional goal, would be includable. The dollar amount reflected under "improvements" would be the difference between the ordinary business or functional cost and the cost of the beauty additive.

Improvements

A long list of positive social benefit items would be established and refined as time went on, with provisions and limitations clearly spelled out. Here is a sampling for a starter.

—Training program for handicapped workers.
—Contribution to black college.
—Extraordinary employee turnover costs generated by minority hiring practices.
—Cost of voluntarily established nursery school for children of employees. (Bonus credits might be set up if expanded beyond the corporation to the community at large.)
—Cost of voluntarily reclaiming and landscaping unsightly dump on company property.
—Cost of voluntarily installing pollution-control devices on factory smokestacks.
—Cost of voluntarily detoxifying finishing-product waste.
—Salary of vice-president on loan for government service to Product Safety Commission.
—Cost of substituting lead-free paint for previously used poisonous lead paint in products or facilities exposed to children.

Detriments

Negative SEOS items would be spelled out in the same manner:

—Postponed installation of cutting machine safety device required to reduce employee hazard (dollar amount of the equipment would be reflected).
—Cost that would have been incurred had strip mining site been relandscaped.
—Estimated cost of purification process, which, for the benefit of the environment, should have been installed to neutralize poisonous discharges into local waterways.
—Cost of product safety innovation, recommended by Safety Council, but ignored by the company.
—Refusal of management to join other members of the community's industrial park in contributing executive time to a "businessmen's council" organized to improve employment opportunities in the area—cost of the time not contributed.

SEOS FORMAT

"Improvements" and "detriments" representing positive and negative social actions and omissions might be broken down into three groups on the SEOS exhibit: relations with people, relations with the environment, relations with products and services.

By way of illustration, I have designed a sample Socio-Economic Operating Statement that might be used as a guide in formulating an "official" model and initiating the SEOS on a nationwide basis.

The response to the SEOS concept thus far varies from person to person, depending on occupation, measure of social con-

JONES CORPORATION
SOCIO-ECONOMIC OPERATING STATEMENT
for the year ended December 31, 1972

I. Relations with People:

  A. Improvements:

    1. Training program for handicapped workers $ 10,000

    2. Contribution to black college   4,000

    3. Extra turnover costs because of minority hiring program   5,000

    4. Cost of nursery school for children of employees, voluntarily set up   11,000

         $ 30,000

  B. Less: Detriments

    1. Postponed installing new safety devices on cutting machines (cost of the devices)   14,000

  C. Net Improvements in People Actions for the Year $ 16,000

II. Relations with Environment:

  A. Improvements:

    1. Cost of reclaiming and landscaping old dump on company property $ 70,000

    2. Cost of installing pollution-control devices on Plant A smokestacks   4,000

    3. Cost of detoxifying waste from finishing process this year   9,000

  Total Improvements $ 83,000

sciousness and concern, and degree of sophistication. Some typical reactions:

Manager (in socially irresponsible corporation): "Interesting, but nobody will use it."

President (of socially responsible company): "Something like this is bound to be adopted in the not too distant future."

Magazine editor: "An exciting prospect. I can promise you that my book will support it all the way."

"Typical" wage earner: "It would be wonderful if you could get business to cooperate. But how does one make a big corporation. . . ?"

Young politician (age 33): "Not only is something like SEOS needed—it is definitely on the way."

B. Less: Detriments			
1. Cost that would have been incurred to relandscape strip mining site used this year	$ 80,000		
2. Estimated cost to have installed purification process to neutralize poisonous liquid being dumped into stream	100,000	$180,000	
C. Net Deficit in Environment Actions for the Year			($ 97,000)
III. Relations with Product:			
A. Improvements:			
1. Salary of V.P. while serving on government Product Safety Commission	$ 25,000		
2. Cost of substituting lead-free paint for previously used poisonous lead paint	9,000		
Total Improvements		$ 34,000	
B. Less: Detriments			
1. Safety device recommended by Safety Council but not added to product		22,000	
C. Net Improvements in Product Actions for the Year			$ 12,000
TOTAL SOCIO-ECONOMIC DEFICIT FOR THE YEAR			($ 69,000)
Add: Net Cumulative Socio-Economic Improvements as of January 1, 1972			$249,000
GRAND TOTAL NET SOCIO-ECONOMIC ACTIONS TO DECEMBER 31, 1972			$180,000

Association official: "It's about time someone came out with a formal proposal to get this thing launched. It's certainly no less urgent than our conventional financial statements."

Obviously, the SEOS does not represent a panacea for our nation's ills. But it is in my view an important ingredient for recognizing social action and inaction. And it is practical and achievable. For one thing, the tempo of the times and political pressures already being brought to bear will militate strongly in its favor. Public concern will continue to mount as massive and costly programs produce grandiose promises and minuscule results and as corporate pledges may not always add up to effective action.

With each passing week, reports in the press and over the airwaves warn us that we edge closer to social disaster. And with each passing week the public grows more mindful of the peril. Citizens rich and poor, young and old, are increasingly shaken by the health implications of fouled air and streams and the personal security implications when desperate citizens are in revolt. As dissension becomes more and more organized and more and more articulate—a phenomenon we see evidenced by new consumer groups, black power groups, feminine power groups, gay power groups, labor groups, taxpayer groups, conservationist groups, and disadvantaged citizen groups—the pressures will build to replace promises with meaningful action.

Society's victims, whatever their status and standing, are learning how to use the tools of protest—the boycott, the traffic bloc, in extreme cases the riot and the bomb. And most important of all, the vote.

Despite its extremists, society's greatest hope for salvation rests with the potential that may be brought to bear through public awareness and public enlightenment. I am talking about the kind of potential that controls huge blocs of votes, the kind of potential to which politicians respond.

I believe that within ten years Socio-Economic Operating Statements or their equivalent will be as familiar to many business organizations as the cash flow statement is today. The exhibits will be prepared by internal interdisciplinary committees and audited by external socio-economic groups. They will be demanded by public interest councils and committees, which are springing up throughout the nation, by politicians with fingers on the public pulse, by regulatory agencies responding to public and political pressures.

The push toward increased public visibility of business activities is already under way. Evidence of this can be seen from coast to coast. One social activist research group, the Council on Economic Priorities, recently listed more than 35 companies facing proxy proposals and other protest tactics from some 13 activist groups. Although none of the groups expect enough votes on their proxy proposals to win, they are looking for the impact that the public exposure of an issue can generate.

The clergy are up in arms too. An Episcopalian council has joined with four other Protestant groups to form the Church Project on U.S. Investments in South Africa. It asked IBM, Gulf Oil, Mobil Oil, and Goodyear for detailed reports of corporate activities in the area. Should a company refuse to respond, the plan is to raise the question publicly at stockholder meetings. As of this writing, IBM and Mobil have agreed to comply.

The Ralph Nader—endorsed Project on Corporate Responsibility has extended its coverage from General Motors to include Chrysler, Ford, AT&T, and six drug companies as well, with these organizations now set on the public block. One objective is to fill board vacancies with women and representatives of employee organizations, consumer groups, and minority groups. Another is to get drug companies to analyze the impact on drug abuse of their pharmaceutical promotion and marketing policies.

In Dayton, Ohio, Gulf lost out on a $56,650 bid to supply oil to the city because it refused to report the number of blacks it employed in the area as required by municipal procurement rules.

The Minneapolis-based Council for Corporate Review has targeted in on Honeywell Inc., Control Data Corp., and Sperry Rand Corporation, among others. It submits proxy proposals to convert defense operations to civilian-oriented production and keeps the public abreast of developments.

I am convinced that not only are SEOS exhibits on their way, but before too long profit organizations will be required to prepare Socio-Economic Operating Budgets to project what the company plans to do in the social area for the coming year.

Congress should enact legislation allowing companies a deduction against taxable income for net social expenditures shown on the SEOS for the year that exceed a certain percentage of the taxpayer's net worth. I would recommend that net socio-economic expenditures that exceed 1 percent of the net worth of a company be allowed as a full deduction from taxable income. This would be in addition to all other expense and depreciation allowances already made for these same items. By such a tax consideration business would further be encouraged and stimulated to undertake large-scale activities to help correct the many abuses in our society and our environment. And it would furnish progressive management with another argument against those of economist Milton Friedman's school who believe that business should be concerned only with dollar profits.

Why devote this chapter to business? The overlap between private and public sector activities is too obvious to describe. To a large extent, business enterprise dominates our society and prescribes its direction. We talk at length about measurement and reporting within the social sector. The discussion would not be complete without including the private sector as well.

We must be practical, too. The great business leaders of this nation could not be expected to disregard the impact of corporate investment, which, however beneficial to society, might reflect adversely on current earnings statements. It would be too much to ask. Even the most farsighted chief executive must to some degree be concerned with his present profit-producing image.

What socially responsible management needs is a meaningful measure of its contributions to society for all of the world to examine and assess. Viewed side by side with the profit and loss statement, it would present a more honest and comprehensive picture of a company's activities.

12

WITHIN OUR GRASP: SURVIVAL PLUS

Society's needs, screaming to be fulfilled, have been amply documented. We know what has to be done. Only one question remains: Can we do it?

Indeed we can. America's potential for survival is the bright hope. Our manpower, brainpower, and sophistication have been demonstrated repeatedly. They have been demonstrated by the strides we have made and are continuing to make in conquering the ocean depths and the reaches of space. They have also been demonstrated by our giant corporations in terms of earnings and growth, in terms of response to market demands for increasingly diverse products and services, and, more recently, in terms of effective action in the area of corporate contribution to social improvement.

What's more, however isolated the examples, we have seen ample evidence of accomplishment potential given the imagination and resolve in the social sector as well. In these chapters we have cited a small sampling of the programs that are producing dramatically successful results in education, housing, health care, crime control, and a host of other fields.

The tools and technology? These too have been tested and proven. We have seen what the computer can do to make some model hospitals and health complexes across the nation more efficient and responsive to community needs. We have seen the computer's potential in optimizing our airlines' reservation systems, apprehending criminals, rescuing ships in distress, plotting the paths of rockets and missiles.

We have seen how, through the use of sophisticated techniques of data capture, retrieval, and analysis, "think tank" groups can determine the intentions of such foreign powers as the Soviets and Chinese, develop models for planning the infinitely complex logistics of troop movements and facilities placements, and design weaponry to a point of ultimate efficiency and maximum "kill power."

If we can achieve maximum kill power, we can achieve maximum needs fulfillment as well. The powerful tools of planning, decision making, budgeting, auditing, measurement, and information handling and reporting have been developed and applied by business executives, accountants, managers, and other professionals with gratifying results. They are all on hand, ready to be applied to the problems of society as well.

And the tools aren't new. Some of them have been around for decades. They've been tested, reworked, and refined. For one, the planning-programming-budgeting system has been demonstrated repeatedly in the military and elsewhere in quantitative areas. Under PPBS, a rigorous analysis is made of competing and conflicting goals, with alternatives selected and funded on a functional or program basis. It can also be used for qualitative measurements.

Another prime example is systems analysis. As former Assistant Secretary of Defense Charles J. Hitch once pointed out, it provides the analytical foundation for the making of sound objective choices among the alternative means of carrying out major military missions. The secretary of defense, he adds, now has the tools he needs to take the initiative in the planning and direction of the entire defense effort on a truly unified basis.

If the secretary of defense can be armed with this capability in quantitative dimensions, why not the secretary of health, education, and welfare in qualitative dimensions? Why not our nation's hospital administrators, poverty program directors, university presidents, penologists, and social and urban planners?

The capability for survival plus embodied in the precepts of Socio-Economic Management is already on hand. The only challenge that remains is to apply it.

THE WATTS THAT MIGHT HAVE BEEN

Armchair hypothesizing is unpopular with those who live in the ghettos and barrios of our nation's larger cities. This nation's hope-shorn millions are understandably incensed and frustrated by endless years of empty promises, scholarly dissertations, and journalistic theories that have done little to date to relieve starvation of either the belly or the mind. Nor do pat remedies for the Wattses of America exist.

I should say at the outset that "The Watts That Might Have Been," here presented, is proposed not as a cure-all but purely for its directional value. As has been stated throughout the book, social reform and solutions for the ghettos are vastly more than one-man, one-agency, or one-program endeavors. They require the harmonized effort and cooperation of multidisciplinary professionals working closely with the disadvantaged they hope to serve and dedicated to the fulfillment of common and well-defined goals.

Still, we need a launching point. In Watts, although here and there a sprinkling of progress has been made since the 1965 holocaust, the situation is worse today than it ever was. Unemployment has risen sharply since the days of the riot. Charcoal Alley is still an unsightly shambles. Bands of jobless youths, eyes burning with hatred and bitterness, still roam the streets restlessly or meet in dark doorways to plan holdups and muggings. The principal commercial enterprises of the deteriorating community continue to be the bail bond offices and the pawnshops.

Dialogue, for all its inability to bring hope to the hopeless, does shed light and understanding. We learn from experience, and from Watts we have learned plenty. In the main we understand *why* this desperate roach- and vermin-infested community, less than a 30-minute ride from posh Beverly Hills, exploded as it did into riot, looting, and mayhem.

We understand, too, that not one of us in the so-called Establishment remains unaffected by what happened in Watts during the 1965 rebellion—for that's what it was—and by what is happening, and failing to happen, in Watts today. For there are not many of us who do not have a potential Watts just

182 STRATEGIES FOR SURVIVAL

a rock's throw from our own backyard. And mounting evidence indicates that the rock piles are being supplemented and reinforced in core cities across the nation by arsenals of handguns, shotguns, automatic rifles, and other weapons of war to a rapidly increasing degree.

Even those of us who are less affected by the screams from our ghettos will be hard put to remain untouched by the chilling prospect of future riots that could produce hundreds of lives lost instead of 34 and billions in damage instead of $40 million. As one black militant recently warned: "The next time around, baby, will make August 1965 seem like a Sunday school picnic."

So what happens now? Though ominously gray, the picture is not all black. One phenomenon did occur after 1965 that before was rare. We *listened*. Despite the general hopelessness, intelligent and articulate spokesmen have come out of Watts. They have told us what they feel, what they need, what has to be done. Which takes us again to the launching pad. Where do we start?

By applying the proven methods of business management to the problems of the ghetto? Yes, to a point. But there's more to it than that.

The uniqueness of the ghetto situation adds a dimension that cannot be ignored. If General Motors, for example, had to operate in the atmosphere of blatant bitterness, mistrust, political legerdemain, and racial tension that prevails in the ghetto, there is little question that its track record would be much less impressive.

On the other hand it has been said that a manager is a manager—and there's much truth to the statement. It would be an oversimplification to say that if you can run a business successfully you can run a city or a nonprofit agency successfully. But as we have noted throughout this book, important parallels exist. Without effective planning, goal setting, decision making, organization, funding, measurement, and evaluation, neither a profit-making nor a nonprofit enterprise could be run successfully. The basics of management apply to all kinds of enterprise. Where they are applied successfully, the chances of getting the desired performance are multiplied.

There is nothing new about this concept. But as has been pointed out, in the great majority of nonprofit endeavors today —including the restructuring of Watts—the basic tenets of management are being largely ignored.

That is where Socio-Economic Management comes into the picture. Adhering to the ten SEM precepts outlined in this book will establish a strong foundation on which to build a viable Watts and a viable society. Without such a foundation, no matter how much money, manpower, or talent we allocate to our ghettos, they will continue to shame us, to fester and seethe.

How might Socio-Economic Management be applied to Watts? Suppose if, back in 1965, and before 1965, southern Los Angeles had been structured with an SEM base in mind. What would have happened? Perhaps the riots would not have occurred. When you remove the powder and take away the fuse, an explosion cannot take place.

My purpose is not to try to propose solutions to great problems, but only to help point the way. In my world of business and organizational management I daily witness what the precepts outlined in this book can achieve in the way of performance and fulfillment. I hope the following will provide some insights into how the situation might have been altered had SEM been applied to Watts.

**Application of rule 1: Tie standards and goals
to proven human needs**
Any program that ever succeeded began with a need. In successful enterprise, where needs are identified, goals are set up, resources allocated, standards of performance established to insure progress, and the program then monitored and evaluated on an ongoing basis.

Not so in Watts. Watts exploded into flaming terror because needs, however well identified, obviously were not responded to in the above-prescribed manner. The evidence speaks for itself. In 1965 not one hospital was operating within the Watts community. Ambulance service was virtually nonexistent. Babies stricken with pneumonia or bitten by rats died because they could not be rushed to medical aid in time. A Watts mother has at least one thing in common with a mother in Beverly Hills. She loves her children. To anyone who has lost a child due to neglect and indifference, the hurling of rocks in response does not seem quite so horrendous.

Job opportunities in Watts? They were scarce in 1965, and are even scarcer today because of the decline of the aerospace industry in southern California. Manufacturers, discouraged by excessive insurance rates, avoid the area. Compounding the problem is a creaking transportation system that traps inhabitants in the ghetto, making outside employment largely inaccessible. One Watts resident, who worked at a steady job for eleven years and is now unemployed due to massive plant layoffs, tells of having spent more than four hours daily getting to and from work, changing buses three times each way.

Education, the ultimate key to higher standards and values and a greater understanding, is no better. Approximately 50 percent of tenth graders drop out of high school before graduating. Graduation itself leaves much to be desired. Says one black 19-year-old: "Graduation to what, man?" Educators, as a writer in a Watts workshop set up by author Budd Schulberg points out, are simply inadequate to the task of teaching in Watts or in any other black ghetto. "A B.A.," he says, "does not qualify one to teach a child who suffers not only from an intellectual starvation, but from a moral starvation. This starvation begins in homes where Mother is seldom there and Daddy's name is only a ghost of a memory, and often cursed by Mother at that."

The list could go on to encompass all important human needs. In the Watts of 1965, block upon block of dismal, dilapidated, officially designated substandard buildings infested with vermin and rodents lay rotting and crumbling. The situation is no different today.

We know well why Watts exploded! It exploded because of joblessness and hopelessness, lack of medical care, moral and intellectual starvation, homes not fit for human habitation. It was exploded by people who had "had it."

Property damage during the Watts riots has been estimated at $40 million. Many times this amount has since been poured into rehabilitation for the troubled community. But rehabilitation has yet to occur. Isn't it reasonable to assume that if these millions were invested in goal-directed efforts instead of on a dispersed basis that the situation might have been ameliorated?

Application of rule 2: Apply funding by results

I know of no truly realistic accounting of the millions that have been allocated to restructure Watts. In 1968 alone some $200 million sloshed over Watts, up $5 million since 1965. A July 1967 *Life* report asserted that 51 percent of the money poured into Watts since the riots had gone for "administration." The writer added: "The ghetto has become a gigantic pork barrel, a place where antipoverty opportunists can get rich quick and split." Another prober quoted a black self-help administrator as commenting: "Man, it was something to see. All you had to do was stick your hand out a window and somebody would put a basket of money in it."

Planned, managed funding? It doesn't sound that way.

The situation is different today. The tap has all but stopped flowing and the "entrepreneurs" are seeking different opportunities. But good efforts as well as bad have ground to a halt and for Watts's 500,000 citizens the prospects look bleaker than ever. At least two-thirds of the area's poverty organizations have closed up shop, according to *Business Week*. Most of the rest are shells. Operation Bootstrap, once highly touted, now has trouble scraping up $8,000 a year. Its training center, which once processed 100 students, is down to fewer than ten. One reason given: "There are too many experienced and trained jobless around now."

Obvious or not, one cannot argue with the reality that successful enterprises fund by results. The technique, long developed, long tested, long proven, is the only kind of funding that makes sense. It works for departments, divisions, and plants. It works for institutions, agencies, and programs. Produce and you get the money to continue and expand, whether your specialty is manufacturing or research, poverty or crime control. Fail to produce and your operation is terminated, cut back, or turned over to a new manager.

It starts, of course, with the machinery of measurement and evaluation (see SEM Rule 1). Once this is set in motion so that management can ascertain how well the program is doing, funding by results is the only effective way to manage money. Experience has repeatedly indicated that where the funding system is not set up to reward excellence and penalize mediocrity, almost invariably mediocrity wins out and political hornswoggling prevails.

Application of rule 5: Set up social profitability audits
Even the best-navigated corporate ships sometimes run off course. The modern company is continually audited not only financially, but also in an effort to spot weaknesses in management performance, policy, and goals and to identify profit opportunities that may exist. For social programs we need socioeconomic audits to verify that the resources are going to advance the true purposes of the programs.

An experienced interdisciplinary team is skilled at the art of pinpointing the performance and structural gaps that help defeat goals. Watts in 1965 and Watts today have not been exposed to a socio-economic audit of the type described. If the community had been examined in terms of social profitability (the fulfillment of human needs), glaring deficiencies would have long ago been spotted and remedial action started.

Perhaps the most challenging lack of all is the failure to attract industry to the area in order to reduce the jobless rate. The reasons for the failure would have been made abundantly clear by a competently managed social profitability audit. After the riots, it would have underlined the futility of pouring millions of dollars into job training for nonexistent jobs. As Booker Griffen of Westminster Neighborhood Association, one of Watts's most effective grass-roots groups, points out: "We were dealing with that social-work philosophy of job training —to prepare people for disappearing jobs."

When a significant attempt to overcome this problem was finally made in 1968, other significant factors were ignored. The effort itself was laudable: to lure labor-intensive industry to the fringes of Watts in order to provide 2,400 jobs for ghetto residents. The program, a 60-acre industrial park, was established by the federally funded Economic Resources Corporation. But after three years and millions of dollars, only one major corporation—Lockheed Aircraft Corp., bailed out of hock by the government—was in residence. The venture, as a socio-economic audit would have predicted, was apparently doomed from the start. Industrial organizations are in business to make money. If they lose money, they want no part of Watts. Why should they, if, for example, insurance rates are double those of more desirable nearby areas? An interdisciplinary SEM audit would have established the critical need for incentives to offset the high rates and other disadvantages of doing business in a surly ghetto continuously threatened by violence.

This kind of audit would also have pointed up the importance of shoring up the community's obsolete and overtaxed transportation system, which makes outside employment inaccessible to Watts residents who do not own cars.

Suppose a system of social profitability audits had been installed. Critics might argue that even if management, policy, and structural failings were identified and corrective action suggested in jobs, housing, education, and a host of other areas, where would the money come from to achieve reform?

What about the millions already poured into Watts? What do we have to show for it? What about the staggering toll caused by violence and riots? What about the millions of dollars in relief being doled out to Watts inhabitants today?

And perhaps most significantly, what about the perils of tomorrow? Undoubtedly, policy control and riot response have been improved since 1965. But is this our total answer? The fuse that set off the August burning and killing is no longer today than it was then. The merest incident—an accidental shooting, a minor arrest, a confrontation between a policeman and a black—could touch it off again. One day in Watts a black man showed a reporter a .45 caliber submachine gun. "There were 99 more in the shipment," he said, "and they are spread around to 99 guys."

Can we afford the high financial cost of social reform in the Wattses of America? The question answers itself when we consider the alternatives.

Application of rule 7: Prune and restructure for dynamic growth

It has been demonstrated time and again that the more complex the endeavor, the greater the need for a well-structured approach for both coping with the situation and attempting a solution. It would be difficult in this day to find a tougher, more complex situation than Watts. In 1965 the only things clear were the desperation of its half million residents, the hopelessness of their outlook, the futility of scattered efforts to reform working and living conditions.

In 1965 a handful of makeshift groups, some of them manned by overworked, earnest, and dedicated crusaders, were struggling against staggering odds to bring a semblance of hope and self-help to the community. There were small successes here and there. But it was like running a treadmill. Drug use mounted steadily; the crime rate climbed; housing continued to deteriorate; the obsolete transportation system left the ghetto ever more isolated. The rate of desperation, in short, rose faster than the improvement.

From government, as bitter Wattsians are fond of pointing out, came studies and promises followed by studies and promises. Goals of the so-called action groups were tenuous and ill-defined. Where reform attempts were honest and well-conceived, they were largely uncoordinated and bogged down by endless red tape.

Inevitably came the riots. After the riots, it was suddenly a new ball game.

"Organizations sprang up like weeds," *Newsweek* reported, "to meet the challenge of gobbling up all the loot. . . . As long as the money flowed, the organizations thrived."

Another investigation discloses that 88 major studies of everything from plumbing to probation were launched. More than 300 organizations ranging from "Operation Escape String" to "Operation Cereal Bowl" cropped up to wage war on poverty and racial tension. The area was invaded by hordes of career reformers. As Eugene Brooks, a young black architect who heads a Watts-based urban workshop, told a prober: "It was quite a phenomenon. Man, every night at 5 P.M. there was a traffic jam on 103rd Street as all the social workers ran home to the suburbs."

Millions of dollars worth of coolant was hosed onto Watts during those early postriot days, not to mention all the home-grown crusaders who poured their hearts and souls into bootstrap efforts and programs. Unfortunately, however, it was like a Three Stooges scenario.

If you'd like a reenactment, line up a thousand carpenters, plumbers, electricians, masons, diggers, crane operators, and riggers. Select a site for a 30-story building, then tell your crew, "All right, fellows, let's go."

The result would be Watts: planless enterprise, confused objectives, new programs superimposed on foundationless endeavors, overlapping functions and work duplication, inefficiency, heart-sickening waste. Not to mention the milking and the corruption. What it all adds up to is nonorganization.

Here is an interesting research project someone might conduct. Let him try to make a depth investigation of the programs, projects, and groups that were formed in Watts on the heels of the riots. Using the corporate style, he should then write up an organizational assessment of each endeavor, detailing the goals of each group, recording the financial and manpower resources thrown into each program, and recapping the results.

However intriguing, it would be a formidable if not impossible task. For typically, where nonorganization exists, accurate records and documented proof of measurement and evaluation are hard to come by.

Consider the talent, the millions of dollars, the sweat and dedication already poured into Watts. Imagine what could have happened if this had been done on a well-organized, centrally controlled and coordinated basis, with the essentials of organization—planning, goal setting, monitoring, standards, measurement, and the rest—making it possible to sort out the positive efforts from the self-serving and politically motivated efforts. This approach could very well have brought about the success everyone had hoped for.

Application of rule 8: Vary the input mix

When military field maneuvers don't work, an imaginative commander devises new tactics. When a political campaign doesn't produce expected results, old methods are discarded and new methods tried. When corporate programs designed to penetrate a market fail, new programs are developed and tested.

Watts, for the main part, keeps spinning its wheels. In 1965 it was apparent to the interested observer that whatever programs were in force, they were producing no more than a minor impact on the overall condition of desperation and hopelessness.

Certainly housing was no better than it had been in the past. The prospects for employment were bleak. The high school dropout rate was high and increasing. The crime rate was at a record peak. There was little evidence of success in keeping youths off the streets and out of trouble. Ghetto inhabitants mistrusted and hated the police.

The reports of observers today echo 1965 reports. Programs didn't work then. They are not working now.

Social programs, as was pointed out earlier, must be regarded as products with social values. A variety of inputs must be tried, the failures filtered out, the successes refined and expanded. There is little evidence of major experimentation in Watts. Where important attempts were made, they were usually stifled by stubborn resistance or beaten down by political machinations. Funding was hard to come by and now that the post-riot excitement is over, it's even harder to come by.

A number of experiments across the nation have been discussed in this book. Surely Watts is ripe for a few of its own, as it is ripe for some of the innovation that is working well in other ghettos.

We now have teaching methods that deal with the emotions as well as the intellect. If some of these were tried in Watts we might one day measure educational achievement there in terms of knowledge and skills acquired instead of in the number of diplomas ground out.

Ghetto schooling might be started at the age of three or four instead of at five or six. This would help to teach youngsters sound values before harmful ones became too strongly entrenched. And it would get them out of squalid, fatherless homes, which only breed ignorance, hatred, and despair in place of hope.

We talked about industry trade training centers with ghetto ownership and ghetto labor and management. What more fitting environment for this than Watts? American ingenuity could devise a government-sponsored incentive scheme (such as special income tax deductions) that would counteract excessive insurance rates and reward instead of punish companies with the social responsibility and courage to set up shop in the ghettos.

Another job experiment might make work hours more flexible, assign workers a job to do, and reward them for performance—with less stress on punctuality.

Some imaginative experiments have been tried and are being tried in Watts. One, called Basic Car Plan, divides the community into nine units with nine policemen assigned in shifts to each. This narrows the relationship so that, presumably, residents get to know their protectors, and the other way around. Monthly meetings in which patrolmen and citizens participate take up such matters as crime prevention and improved communication. No one pretends the program has gotten rid of the traditional mistrust of police in Watts. But some people are responding. A start has been made.

Another experiment, as costly as it is intriguing, combines high school, junior high, and elementary school in one district of Watts into a single complex. The extra funding cuts teacher loads and provides needed learning materials, adult education facilities, and a skills center for training the hard-core unemployed. Results thus far have been encouraging, especially in upgraded reading and math skills.

Other attempts at innovation—for example, using youngsters to help clean ghetto streets, and transporting youths to work on projects outside the ghetto—show promise of the improvement that might one day be achieved. But significant experiments are too few and far between, and even good experiments will necessarily produce only limited success so long as the proper planning, organization, goal setting, measurement, and evaluation that constitute the total framework of Socio-Economic Management are lacking.

This is a small sample, selected at random, relating SEM precepts to the actual Watts condition. The other rules of SEM are just as applicable.

Application of other rules

Rule 9, stir up social competition, urges that marketplace mechanisms be initiated in the nonprofit sector as incentives to higher standards of performance. As far back as 1967 the late

Senator Robert Kennedy and other legislators were pushing—futilely—for bills that would provide tax incentives for private enterprises locating plants in the ghetto. The absence of such plants today is eloquent proof of our failure to respond to this pressing need.

Rule 4 calls for multidisciplinary planning. Repeated case histories have demonstrated what a depressed community can achieve in the way of progress when managers, accountants, and systems analysts are brought in to work with social planners and administrators. Nor should the importance of grass roots involvement in planning, projects, and programs be overlooked. As one Watts-bred administrator puts it: "The man thinks he knows us. But you don't get to know nothing much on a nine to five basis." Yet a great deal of funding in Watts and other ghettos is still remotely allocated and controlled, with managerial and communications shortcomings as blatant today as they were in the pre-riot days.

The plight of Watts residents has been widely publicized in the press, and in many instances creditable reporting jobs have been done. But in the main, SEM Rule 6, establish public visibility, is still a long way from meaningful implementation. For one thing, the confusion over leadership has never been officially clarified.

We also lack controlled, well-directed public visibility regarding the economics of the Watts situation. Welfare costs there at the time of the riots were five times what they were for the rest of Los Angeles. "We're simply failing to get across to the public," remarks a Watts-assigned economist, "that our failure to allocate the proper resources to the right programs would be the most costly mistake we could make."

Information and reporting today represent no significant strides over 1965. We're still unable to answer most of the crucial questions regarding the extent of employment, health, housing, and educational needs. We have established no reliable base from which progress could be monitored and measured. The most essential question of all: "How are we doing?" is still largely unanswerable, except that from the climate of bitterness and frustration we can judge that the tension has not been reduced.

Nonetheless, many dedicated men and women are pouring their very lifeblood into attempts at improvement in Watts. One ray of hope is a small manufacturing operation called Image, Inc. This growing enterprise, which produces printed circuit boards, employed a handful of Watts residents at its inception and employs a good many more today. It got under way when ten California corporations put up $50,000 each for noncontrolling shares in the company. At last report, it was beginning to turn profitable.

A comprehensive survey and analysis of Watts in 1965 would undoubtedly reveal hundreds of failings that could not have taken place under an effectively installed network of Socio-Economic Management. And since history has taught us time and again that violence stems essentially from frustrated hopes and unfulfilled human needs, it would not be unreasonable to assume that under SEM, in place of the riots we might have seen progress.

RETURN TO BASICS

Sometimes people seem to have a knack for sidestepping the simple and obvious solution and getting snarled in red tape. For hunger, the solution is food. For ignorance, learning. For joblessness, jobs. For sickness, health care.

The remedies we have in abundance. But we are fond of sifting them through complex, unwieldy, politically distorted nonsystems until the end product is watered down, the result of misappropriated and misapplied money and energy.

Socio-Economic Management is founded on the basic principles of planning, operating, and administering enterprise. Perhaps at this point in our history what we need most is a return to basics.

In recent years I undertook several State Department and UN missions to Southeast Asian and European countries. During these missions to help the developing nations it became abundantly clear to me that essentially these governments have not yet departed from the basics. It is a significant point in their favor. They are thus quicker to grasp the values of the SEM approach than we are in America.

When a developing nation undertakes a five-year plan, it may aim at relieving hunger in a designated sector of, say, 100,000 people, by bringing agricultural development and employment to the area. Dams, roads, schools, fertilizer plants, and other facilities will all be planned with this one main objective in view. And until the target population is gainfully employed, the program is not considered complete or successful. The building of a factory, dam, or transportation system would not be bureaucratized into an independent entity divorced from the stated goal.

Interestingly, in some of the developing nations of the world —largely, I believe, as a result of their simple acceptance of and faith in the basics of sound management principles—I have seen strides made and goals achieved that we in America, for all our sophistication and expertise, would be hard put to match.

Under an established democratic bureaucracy overorganized into unwieldiness, objectives are often confused. Functions overlap. Effort is duplicated. A developing nation, because it is eager to accelerate development, more often relies on centralized planning for the allocation of resources and the fulfillment of goals.

The advantages of this simplified approach are clear. It avoids the kind of fragmented effort we see today in most of our social institutions. It focuses on needs and on the performance required to meet them.

In America today we play a complex money game, a game in which our social problems have outdistanced our ability to buy solutions. What is more, intense competition exists for what limited public dollars are available for social use. It is a kind of monetary roulette, and it leads to ruin.

More money alone will not solve our problems. It is the way we spend the money that counts. And a change in priorities is only part of the need. More basic is the organizational system and structure within which the priorities are set up.

THE PROVEN WHEREWITHAL

Can we do the job that is needed for survival plus? I think we can. We have proven it often enough.

We have developed objective-based standards and management techniques in our plants and offices that generate the performance and productivity required for commercial success in the world's most fiercely competitive free enterprise system. Can we afford to settle for less in the social sector?

In industry, we have sharpened and refined the ability to fund by results and allocate resources in proportion to our return on investment. Can we afford to sink billions into social programs with total disregard of the benefits received?

We call on the full gamut of professional skills in the waging of war, the conquest of space, and the operation of business. Can we afford to ignore these capabilities in the planning and management of our social institutions?

We use the tested and proven tools of auditing and evaluation in our business enterprise to spot management and operational shortcomings before they can undermine corporate objectives. Can we afford to jeopardize the social objectives essential to survival by our failure to monitor and assess performance effectively?

In industry, we have been able to establish the kind of visibility that is required for effective communication and the proper setting of priorities. Can we afford to bypass the public visibility that will aid in the establishment of goals, allocation of resources, and election of leaders?

We have demonstrated our ability to respond to the organizational needs of corporate enterprise by merger, divestiture, and pruning where they are required to add structural strength or shore up weaknesses. Can we afford, in the social sector, to perpetuate the obsolete and overorganized institutions that help to breed failure and sap our resources?

We have developed in a nation that was founded on ingenuity and that boasts the world's most eloquently successful experiment in free democracy the ability to boost sales, penetrate new markets, reduce operating costs, and make better products faster as a result of imagination and innovation. Can we afford to tolerate stultification in the planning and administration of our social programs and agencies?

We have produced an outstandingly successful economy based largely on the achievement of excellence through free competition in the marketplace. Can we afford to hogtie social growth by limiting and restricting options in such primary services as housing, education, and health care?

The evidence speaks for itself. America possesses all the human and financial resources it needs to create an economy so fruitful our past accomplishments would seem small by comparison. Survival plus is well within our grasp. But it will not come automatically. Nor will it come by wishful thinking or good intentions alone.

It will come in one way only—through the public-supported effort of applying sound management principles to the work of social scientists and public administrators. It will come through the coordinated implementation of the ten rules outlined in this book—however obvious they may seem. It will come in a nationwide turnaround that could be unprecedented in the history of a nation's institutions.

This, then, is our blueprint for survival. Socio-Economic Management is, I believe, an idea whose time has come. It is an idea that must be adopted now—if the future of our democracy as we know it is to be assured.

13

THE SPECIFICS
FOR SURVIVAL

The strategies for survival outlined in this book are apparently catching on. But their application to date has been loose, fragmented, uncoordinated. The question is will SEM be integrated *in time* into the nation's socio-economic structure? Some of the signs are encouraging.

There is a growing awareness that the problems nagging most of our social institutions today are primarily problems of management. The parallels between corporate and noncorporate management are becoming more and more pronounced. A classic example of this is New York University's experience in its ongoing battle for economic survival.

A *Business Week* editor wrote that NYU discovered the economics of a big university resemble those of a corporation. There are rising costs, a shifting market, too much dependence on government money, and the unforeseen business conditions that can make a mockery of the best laid plans.

More encouraging is the fact that the critical need to apply such SEM principles as goal setting in response to identified needs, measurement, organizational pruning, incentives, and controls is now being recognized at the highest levels of government. President Nixon's appointment of Roy L. Ash, former president of Litton Industries, as director of the Office of Management & Budget is eloquent proof of this. In essence, the application of SEM principles—or whatever Ash may choose to call them—will be his No. 1 responsibility. Added proof is Caspar W. Weinberger's appointment to succeed Elliot Richardson as secretary of Health, Education and Welfare. HEW has long been regarded as an unequaled governmental example of overpriced and underperforming social action programs. Well-intentioned or not, such programs are in desperate need of reassessment and restructuring. Weinberger's role has been categorized as that of a "sympathetic ax wielder," a pruning role well known to innumerable businessmen. I would hope that he will apply the kind of qualitative dimension espoused in the SEM principles as he tackles his pruning role.

So while the application of SEM techniques keeps building, we cannot afford so slow a pace. Viewed in the broad perspective, SEM application has been infinitesimal. Huge numbers of agencies and costly programs are still being "managed" as they were decades ago, with billions of taxpayer dollars flushed down the drain as a consequence and problems no closer to solution. On the other hand, the evidence of what can be accomplished when SEM is properly applied has become too overwhelming to dismiss.

Success is the world's most effective persuader. What follows is a rundown of concrete examples of SEM successfully applied. It is to be hoped it will provide some insight into America's achievement potential at such time as SEM becomes universally applied in an organized and integrated manner.

SCHOOL PARTNERSHIP PROGRAM

Approximately 49 percent of black and 55 percent of Spanish-speaking ninth graders leave New York City high schools before graduation, a disquieting waste of human resources. Sharing this belief is the Economic Development Council of New York City, an independent, nonprofit organization established in 1965 to "bring the capabilities of business to bear on vital urban problems." It accomplishes this goal by "loaning" executives on an extended full-time basis to institutions in need. Working in teams of three or four, the executives apply tested management principles to the organizations they serve.

EDC's "school partnership" program was structured to address the problems of disruption, student morale, and dropouts at four New York high schools: George Washington, Bushwick, James Monroe, and Brandeis. A key purpose of the program is to achieve the "multiplier effect"—the development of projects that will prove applicable not only in New York schools but nationwide.

In the partnership program, EDC teams worked much the same way as corporate task force groups. Step one was a feasibility study at each of the four schools. This involved defining problems as they were perceived by administrators, teachers, students, parents, and community leaders. In any organization, the identification of needs must precede the setting of goals.

The approach pays off in corporate troubleshooting; it also pays off in social troubleshooting. George Washington High is a case in point. Tensions ran high there in the fall of 1970. During that period, GW was shut down 20 percent of the time due to student disruption. One in-school riot overflowed onto the streets and subways, and 34 people were injured.

Committing itself to a partnership agreement at this school was a high risk decision for EDC. It was made nonetheless. The reasoning: If GW could be turned around, so could any other school in the country.

The team worked with educators, students, and parents to locate the storm centers, principally the school cafeteria and the security system in general. Problems were defined and goals spelled out. The next step was to develop projects designed to boost morale, eliminate disruption, and keep the school operational on a full-time basis. A plan for faster cafeteria service was developed. More attractive menus were prepared. An effective student-teacher patrol was initiated. With the assistance of industry specialists, school security was analyzed and new definitions of duties and responsibilities drawn up.

That was part one of the restructuring. Part two involved the "turned off" students, always the most troublesome. A major objective was to turn them back on. The first step was the so-called prep school program, which was set up to deal with selected problem students. A group of volunteer teachers was organized to work with these youngsters on a highly individualized and personal basis.

During the earlier "reign of terror," GW's athletic programs had collapsed. The gym, the swimming pool, and the athletic fields had become dangerous places to frequent. Football had been called off. To reactivate it, the task force helped promote a community drive to raise funds, hire coaches, and provide equipment. In the fall of 1971 a squad of 85 was on field. Crowds came, cheerleaders cavorted, school spirit was renewed.

Sparked in large measure by a progressive and aggressive new principal, other projects were soon launched. A student-parent-faculty communications system was revived. An "English-as-a second-language" program was established for the 55 percent of GW students whose native tongue is not English. An automotive laboratory with a real car and real parts was set up to interest and motivate students. A drug education program was initiated. A film-course library was set up, as was a school and career articulation program. All programs were targeted to address real student needs.

The results have been impressive. Since January 1971 George Washington has been open and fully functioning. Average daily attendance of prep school students has shot up from 15 percent to 90 percent. Whereas only 10 percent of these students had passing grades in the main school, 60 percent passed all subjects at Prep and 20 percent failed in only one subject. The remaining 20 percent failed in two.

Among low-achiever athletes, averages rose from 57 to 70 percent. Semester absences in this group fell from an average of 30 to three. Drug addiction has been substantially reduced by the drug education program.

Significant gains were reported in other schools as well. At Monroe High, 22 teachers met with the management specialists. They analyzed the system, set objectives, developed and implemented projects, and evaluated program effectiveness. Simulation games—"Word Power," "Make Your Own World," "Starpower," and so forth—a technique used widely in industry, have become an accepted teaching tool at Monroe. The "Brotherhood Establishment" has literally driven drug pushers out of the school. This "peer group" approach has become the model for similar programs now in effect in 30 New York City high schools. Evening tutorial sessions have been launched, along with "industry in the classroom" courses.

At Brandeis High School and at Bushwick, "Operation Call-up" has boosted attendance appreciably. Under this program, a team of paraprofessionals telephone the homes of students with exceptionally poor attendance records—it's as simple as that. At Bushwick, a ghetto school with a high dropout rate, a "Careers and You" program, targeted to specific needs and interests, has done much to improve morale and is now being expanded to all ninth grade classes.

CRIME CONTROL—COOK COUNTRY, ILLINOIS

Crime was on the rise, control costs getting out of hand. The Cook County Commission on Criminal Justice hired the management consulting firm of Cresap, McCormick and Paget to study the County's 124 police departments, the goal being improved management. After a brief preliminary survey, eight police departments were examined in depth. They were treated as if they had been individually contracted for, and a separate report was issued to each.

"The studies were comparable to corporate vertical probes," notes CMP principal William Evans. "When complete, the information was pulled together and applied to the entire police network."

A key question: "What business are you in?" Police chiefs didn't know what to make of it. Though they were 20- and 30-year men, it had never occurred to them. Their standard answer: All cities have police departments, and their job is to control crime.

The consultants found otherwise. Police patrol work is a prime example. Ninety percent of this activity, notes consultant Louis Knapp, deals with citizen calls ranging from barking dogs, loud radios, and cats stuck in trees to noisy children and domestic squabbles. One solution, says Knapp: Have special car units for nonemergency calls, crime patrols for crime response.

Police work, he points out, is a labor-intensive operation. The key to proper manpower utilization lies in effective "demand analysis." He cites an example. The majority of crimes are committed between 4 and 12 P.M. But in most cities studied, police manpower is reduced during this period. Utilization was determined by population and geography, with scant attention paid to workload. It doesn't make sense. A company puts most of its salesmen where demand is the greatest. Social institutions should do the same.

Modern SEM-oriented police departments (Knapp cites St. Louis and Kansas City, Missouri, as examples) are developing techniques to measure demand, thereby determining where and when policemen are needed. Kansas City has assigned 25 men to a planning and research unit. With the help of a computer (not required in smaller cities), the unit can predict where 98 percent of the crime will take place, with manpower allocated accordingly. Specific problems are nailed down as they occur.

One case in point: a rash of taxicab robberies. When this particular crime wave was analyzed it was found that most of the victims were members of a single fleet. Management was consulted. "You're being hit to an unreasonable degree; it looks suspicious," the research unit pointed out. A dictum was laid down to the drivers: "The next man robbed gets fired." It was the end of the problem.

It always boils down to the same question: "What business are you in?" Answer that and the problem is 90 percent solved.

Another manpower-related snag, professional jealousy, existed in virtually all police departments surveyed. Chiefs insist on performing a full range of services whether or not they possess the capabilities to handle them. In one small town where no murder had been committed for 28 years, the police department tackled a complex murder case completely on its own, requesting no outside help. Inevitably, the case was badly bungled.

Both city police and sheriff's departments engage in patrol and detective work. But city patrols, the study found, are far more effective, with average response time (the time it takes a patrol car to arrive on the scene) three minutes, as opposed to 25 minutes for sheriff patrol units. Costs are equally telling: $106,000 per city unit, $278,000 per sheriff unit—obtained by dividing the number of units into the annual budget. On the other hand, city detective units do not function nearly so well as sheriff's-department detective units. The conclusion is obvious: Have city patrol units service neighboring noncity areas; have sheriff's-department detective units service cities as well.

Match the men to the job, one of the most ancient and basic of management axioms.

Another key finding: The city pays for the number of patrol units on the street and available for call. On a typical evening shift, the study showed, more than half the patrols were tied up on routine calls and unavailable. The consultant's recommendation was portable radios for all patrol units. If, in the course of a routine call, a robbery, say, or an attempted rape were reported nearby, the patrolman would race to the scene of the crime. He would return later to wind up the service call. Thus, at minimal cost, the availability of patrol units would be doubled.

"Police departments tend to manage the wrong things," Bill Evans notes. "They look on salaries as part of the budget, fixed and uncontrollable. Yet 90 percent of the crime control cost is personnel. Instead of managing people's time, they're preoccupied with numbers."

Numbers is never the answer. Increasing manpower does not necessarily improve response time, solve crimes, or cut their number. A prime example is Elgin, Illinois (not part of Cook County), where another study was made. A year before the study the detective force had been doubled. Instead of boosting the clearance rate (number of crimes solved), it served to decrease it by 30 percent. Something was obviously wrong.

A management probe disclosed the answer quickly enough. What detectives were doing had little relation to the solving of crimes. They sat in their cars and listened to the radio. In essence, they were beefing up the patrol force and not much more. The system was changed. Detectives got out of their cars. They ran down leads. They performed the leg work and investigation associated with the solving of crimes. At last report clearance had jumped from 19 percent, well below the national average, to 33 percent, well above the national average. The rate is holding up, according to Elgin Police Chief Robert Baird who, as of this writing (December 1972), predicted a year-end clearance rate of between 34 and 35 percent.

The basic management principle involved is that it's more important to be doing the right things than to be doing things right.

No punches were pulled in spelling out problems to Cook commissioners and laying down recommendations. "When we submitted our report," Evans recalls, "we half expected to be thrown out on our ears. We weren't. The commission voted 23 to 0 to accept our recommendations and get them implemented as quickly as possible."

SEWICKLEY (PA.) VALLEY HOSPITAL

In November 1970 the WOFAC Company, a consulting firm, conducted a ten-day study to determine nursing staff requirements through the application of modern management techniques. Findings were typical of those in many public service institutions.

Consultants found work measurement and controls virtually nonexistent. Work distribution was inequitable. Time and care forecast tools were not available so that staff requirements could not be projected in advance. There was no system for defining objectives and evaluating performance to see if goals were being met. Without going through the mechanics, suffice it to say that these inadequacies were remedied and a modern management system installed.

The most impressive result is an annual saving of $103,000 in staff reductions, considerably less than the cost of the study. Outside help no longer has to be summoned when an employee calls in sick. A classification system was set up to match patients and nurses by need. With staffing requirements projected in advance, better manpower utilization has been effected, with the patient a co-beneficiary of the program.

TOTAL DEVELOPMENT CONCEPT—STATE OF MAINE

The chief objective of this long-range program is to reduce the level of unemployment by applying modern production and marketing strategies. Specifically, the state of Maine is trying to create 160,000 new jobs by the end of the decade. Unless this goal is met, many young residents, now students, will be unable to find employment, which will force them to migrate elsewhere, most likely to already heavily congested metropolitan areas.

TDC's prime developer is James Keefe, commissioner of the Department of Commerce and Industry. The program is wide-ranging and still too new to discuss in depth. But one aspect is particularly intriguing—the concept of coordinating and integrating industry efforts in such a way as to optimize individual capabilities. The aim here is to keep profitable companies profitable and shore up marginal employer operations to insure survival and the preservation of jobs.

The first successful use of the concept has been in the wood industries. The Woodchip Project, involving sawmill operators, is a case in point. Initial analysis, which clarified the realities of the lumber business in Maine, revealed that any sawmill that limited itself to the production of lumber alone would face an uncertain market, with prospects of periodic layoffs, if not a shutdown, in the months ahead. Converting to finished products as well would make it possible to build a broader and more secure operating base.

TDC works toward this goal through cooperative industry planning. One aim is to locate complementary facilities—transportation, power, communications, training, housing—sufficiently close together to make material handling and distribution more efficient and less costly. The effect of this is to achieve a more integrated and stable economy. A first step in this direction already has been taken by Woodplex, a lumber-producing concern. A pilot operation is well under way to build this company into a fully integrated wood-manufacturing complex. When this becomes operational, the company's president, Howard Cederlund, anticipates "a significant improvement in the local employment situation."

COMMISSION FOR ADMINISTRATIVE SERVICES IN HOSPITALS (CASH)

The call for increased hospital efficiency is familiar to all. But many hospital administrators feel efficiency works against them. Much of their income stems from third-party payers through cost reimbursement. Under this system, they complain, an inefficient administrator can get as much as, or more than, an administrator who performs efficiently by doing little or nothing to improve productivity.

To correct this situation, Blue Cross, in conjunction with the Social Security Administration and other cooperating groups, launched CASH. Its objective is to make more efficient use of personnel through the application of scientific management techniques.

The program's chief tool—which has long been used by industry to make salesmen more productive and boost plant and office output—is incentive reimbursement. Under CASH, each hospital gets an incentive payment based on savings that result from its labor cost improvement.

Largely experimental, the program to date has met with limited success for a variety of reasons only tentatively defined. With participation voluntary, it hasn't always been easy to find volunteers. Some administrators still equate cost improvement with quality decline. Hospital management must deal with other pressures for the extra dollars. The system is complex and not fully understood. Some administrators have been frightened off by penalties for poor performance. Others have experienced difficulty with industrial engineering standards and work-measurement techniques.

But the concept, inherently valid and managerially sound, is slowly taking hold. For the 235 hospitals that are participating in the California program, Blue Cross's mid-1972 estimates report an annual labor reduction of 925 million hours, a cost saving of $32 million.

This year in Rhode Island, under a new law, the state is taking part in budget negotiations and can approve rates. For all the problems it creates, such involvement can be telling. Rhode Island Hospital cites a saving of about $400,000 through more efficient operation on the heels of initial negotiations. This produced the lowest annual hospital cost boost in the past five years. For the first time in years, Blue Cross did not have to ask for a rate increase. The program is now being expanded to other hospitals in the state.

FOUR CITIES PROGRAM

The advanced management strategy of technology transfer is being applied with outstanding success by large corporations, particularly those in the aerospace industry. William V. Donaldson, who has achieved recognition for his work in transferring technology to the city of Scottsdale, Arizona, has said: "Perhaps the real reason technology transfer from the scientific and professional communities to cities hasn't taken place on a broad basis is because nobody knows how to do it."

"Four Cities" is correcting this fault. In 1971, under this program, cosponsored by the National Science Foundation and industry, four engineers from Lockheed, Northrop, Space-General Co., and TRW were sent to help four city managers—in Fresno, San Jose, Anaheim, and Pasadena—achieve technology transfer. In each case, the engineer has his company's backing as a consultant and maintains close liaison with it. Quarterly progress reports on specific activities go to all four engineers, all city managers, all company representatives, NASA, and the National Science Foundation and Jet Propulsion Laboratory, which is managing the program.

Early reports are exciting. Innovations in Fresno range from new types of fire-fighting equipment and waste-disposal systems to the planning of bicycle paths. In Pasadena, industry audiovisual and management information techniques have been applied to streamline the city's communication system. City departments are being converted to a management by objectives (MBO) system. The MBO premise is that management is most effective when each person is aware of how his tasks fit into overall goals and has committed himself to getting specific jobs done in a specified time.

Each week in San Jose's city hall, Lockheed experts conduct training sessions to teach city staffers new management techniques. And knowledge painfully acquired by spacemen over long years in the development and application of computer systems is being transferred to municipal managers. Similar progress is reported in Anaheim. And in Tacoma—although it is not in the program—a demand-response transportation system (similiar to the police system already described) is in the process of being installed. Its aim is to make traffic routing flexible so that optimum service may be provided when and where it is needed.

The National Science Foundation's response to Four Cities? In the words of its director, Dr. H. Guyford Stever: "One broad observation has been that the cities can greatly benefit from being introduced to the systems approach to problem solving used throughout the aerospace industry."

City managers in Fresno and San Jose already have seen enough of the potential of the systems approach to request that the newly created post of science and technology adviser to the city manager be retained permanently in the city's table of organization.

SAMARITAN HEALTH SERVICES—PHOENIX, ARIZONA

A cardinal SEM principle discussed in Chapter 6 is "prune and restructure for dynamic growth." An important part of dynamic restructuring is the merger of organizational units or agencies where such merger can bring about improved service, economy, and productivity. As has been proved innumerable times in industry, strategic consolidation properly conceived, planned, and implemented is capable of producing group purchasing and utilization gains, consolidation of administrative and professional services, and other economies associated with improved management. How well this can be applied to the social sector has been demonstrated by the 1968 consolidation of eight Phoenix-area hospitals into the Samaritan Health Services system.

A federally financed two-year study of the merger was conducted by Chicago's Health Services Research Center. It revealed that Samaritan managers were able to achieve higher gains in cost containment, comprehensiveness, quality, and availability of care.

To date, the report states, the merger has been a financial success. The average increase in cost per SHS case (1968–1971) was 36.6 percent, as compared to 41.2 percent for the unmerged control hospitals. This, despite the fact that during the same period Samaritan faced considerable start-up costs, added more services than the unmerged control hospitals, and improved quality and availability of health care. Today SHS offers "a significantly greater number of services than other hospitals of similar size and scope." At the 7 smaller hospitals integrated into the 713-bed Samaritan Hospital, 15 of 21 instances of service improvements have been attributed to coordinated management (another term for SEM) and shared financial backing.

Sam A. Edwards, director of the Health Services Research Center, sums up the findings in these words: "The members of the research staff believe that the data collected during the past two years clearly illustrates how hospitals working together in a common corporate structure can do a better job of delivering health care than separate institutions facing all of the financial and other hazards usually found in the single hospital system."

FARMER'S MARKET—CHARLESTON, WEST VIRGINIA

Funding was provided to better the plight of low-income farmers in this depressed agricultural community. Farmers had been unable to find buyers for their produce, and so the Farmer's Market was established to serve as a distribution center.

It was mismanaged from the start. Loans were made to farmers for fertilizer and seed without being recorded. The enterprise lost a considerable sum and wound up a shambles. At this point consultants were called in to help straighten the books, restore record keeping, and set up a management system.

The first step was a management probe of the overall operation. Officials were asked, "What is the market's purpose and function?" ("What business are you in?") The question wasn't well received. "We buy what the farmers produce," the consultants were told. "Without the Farmer's Market, they'd be unable to sell their yield. They're unable to find other markets."

The Farmer's Market was no more successful in disposing of the produce, consultants found. Most of it was dumped. They soon learned why. Production was sparse, growing methods primitive, the quality of the food as poor as it looked. The problem, the consultants concluded, was not distribution, but production. "Fold up the market," they counseled, "it serves no worthwhile end."

At first officials and farmers alike balked at the suggestion. Officials especially liked to point to this tangible evidence that something real and concrete was being done for the farmers. It was a highly visible program. Eventually, however, they were made to see the light. The Farmer's Market was discontinued. Funding was then directed to a program that brought in agricultural experts from the university to work with farmers. They taught them what to grow and when and how to grow it. They taught them, in short, how to do the right thing.

Today, farmers in the area are producing—and successfully marketing—vast quantities of prime-quality tomatoes and other desirable crops. They're still a long way from being prosperous, but their condition has substantially improved.

TENNESSEE EFFECTIVE MANAGEMENT PROGRAM (TEMP)

The purpose of this Blue Cross program is to assist member hospitals in utilizing manpower and resources more effectively. TEMP applies industrial engineering techniques long used by industry to help define and achieve cost containment goals without sacrificing the quality of patient care.

Under the program, participating hospitals hire trained methods analysts, who serve in a consulting capacity. Technology transfer is also involved. Similarities in hospital services and facilities make it possible for TEMP analysts to serve hospitals on a group basis.

A variety of innovations are made. Quality control procedures insure a high performance level. Systems improvements simplify methods. Staffing and scheduling guidelines help department managers determine whether they are properly staffed for the work being done in their units. Management development and supervisory training help insure that modern management techniques will be understood and employed.

Gains to date have been impressive in terms both of better health care service and cost containment. Nursing service has been upgraded and preventive maintenance systems have been installed. Admission procedures have been streamlined, waiting time has been decreased. New equipment-justification reviews have been put into effect. Employee attitude and morale have improved substantially.

"Cost containment results," according to TEMP's 1971–72 annual report, "are primarily related to elimination of unnecessary expenses which are usually related to overstaffing, poor supply control, and/or poor utilization of equipment or space."

If totally implemented, the report continues, TEMP recommendations (a recently installed monitoring system shows about 60 percent implementation) will save the 25 participating members (17 full-time active) an estimated $1,370,000 per year. The amount of saving implemented per dollar of cost is $3.65 per year. With the rate of implementation gradually rising, the potential is encouraging.

COMMUNITY ACTION AGENCY, RICHMOND, VIRGINIA

Management and administration in many of the nation's community action agencies (CAAs), which have been established to relieve poverty, are weak and, in some cases, on the point of foundering. A case in point is the Richmond CAA, where management consultants were invited to conduct a management probe and to recommend a management improvement plan, working with the agency to implement the latter.

CAAs in general face great inherent difficulties, including the lack of cohesiveness in the governing body, the need to employ persons unable to find regular work elsewhere, the disagreement of many citizens with CAA objectives, and the need to carry out complex planning with personnel who lack the proper training and experience.

Few CAAs possess even the basic tools of organization and management. Such rudimentary items as organization charts, position descriptions, financial statements, comprehensive reporting, and personnel procedures are unfamiliar to both policy makers and employees. Consequently, many CAAs are loose associations of individuals operating without any sound rules of the road. Yet a CAA is managerially simple; it does not require sophisticated management techniques, merely the basics. Consequently, it is not difficult to turn a CAA around.

"What we came up with in Richmond," notes one of the consultants, "was typical of what we had run into in the past. The operation was lacking in mission. Neither goals nor plans were set up. Productivity was minimal. Money was being plowed into neighborhood workers. The CAA was organizing the poor instead of helping them."

An early step was to reorganize the board of directors into functional committees, whose goals and purpose were carefully defined. John Chiles, a crusader with missionary zeal and an understanding of poverty problems, was brought in to head up the operation. A former teacher and social worker, Chiles had the leadership qualities needed. All he required was some guidance in structuring and methodology. This was provided.

The CAA staff—formerly consisting of low-paid employees unable to make *themselves* self-sufficient—was completely reorganized. Funds were invested in capable people qualified to gauge program effectiveness and relate progress to goals. Intermediate supervisors, previously lacking, were put in to fill the field-sergeant role of training, evaluation, and discipline.

As one outside adviser notes: "Funds were provided for the planning and analysis functions, to define the business, to define poverty itself, and explore what was feasible. You can't cure everything. You have to pin down the specifics of what can and cannot be done."

What could be done was plenty. By targeting allocations to specific objectives—a key SEM tenet—a track record of success was chalked up. Visibility was established—here's what we can do if given the chance. With public notice achieved, the Richmond CAA, formerly overly dependent on OEO money, was able to diversify its funding inputs. It was also able to launch a "halfway house" narcotics program, to create special training facilities, and to undertake a host of other worthwhile projects.

The Richmond CAA has come a long way since the probe. Today the City of Richmond itself employs the agency on a contractual arrangement—a situation that is almost unique—to conduct manpower training and other programs, and pays an annual fee in excess of $100,000.

KEY FACTOR ANALYSIS

The Raleigh, North Carolina, firm of Jarett, Rader & Long-hurst, which bills itself as "Managers of Organizational Systems," markets and installs a management system called key factor analysis (KFA).

KFA represents both a philosophy of management and a strategy for organizational renewal. Its underlying assumption is that a social organization exists for the sole purpose of meeting the human needs of a definable population. Its basic precepts are simple. One byproduct of the system is an information network designed to serve the organization in such a way that measurable results can be made visible, funding directed to effective projects, and organizational coordination and integrity achieved.

Problems are defined as unmet needs. Goals describe how the problem is to be solved. They are set up as milestones against which the organization can evaluate its progress. A key factor—societal responsibility, for example, or vocational skills in a mental health application—provides a qualitative base for measuring the fulfillment of objectives. It answers the question: "How are we doing?" Key indicators measure the movement within key factors—for example, unemployment rate, relating to vocational skills; or trade school enrollment.

The first user of key factor analysis—this was in late 1968—was the North Carolina Department of Mental Health. The second user was the Fort Logan Mental Health Center in Denver, Colorado.

Initially, in North Carolina, a multidisciplinary task force of 120 people—psychiatrists, accountants, nurses, social workers, psychologists, and other professionals—were divided into teams of 8 to 12. Their job was to define organizational purpose and objectives, outlining key factors and key indicators. They worked under a small directional group headed by Dr. Daniel W. Rader, assistant commissioner of Human Resources, the agency that oversaw the project, coordinating activities and communications. A wealth of valuable data, available but untouched for years, was dredged up and put to practical use.

Later, a task force on social issues was organized to spell out specific goals in terms of results expected. Planning must be a function of management, not something performed by remote "planners" uninvolved in the problems. The criteria for measurement of the goal should be contained within the goal itself, thus making the job of program evaluation a good deal easier.

Frequently, people are deluded into thinking that the cheaper a program is, the more efficient it must be. It is mandatory to measure effectiveness before cost even becomes a relevant factor. With this in mind, a reporting system was designed to make visible four basic measures of progress: (1) organizational efficiency, (2) organizational benefit, (3) program effectiveness, and (4) program efficiency. These four measures provide the conceptual framework for designing the benefit and cost reporting system.

In addition to upgrading the level of mental-health-care delivery in North Carolina, modern management techniques are weeding out inefficiency and waste. It is anticipated, for example, that there will be a 10 to 15 percent reduction in record-keeping costs, now estimated to be as much as 30 percent of the operating budget.

In practical terms, how well does the system work? The story of one community project director, Billy Witherspoon, is a case in point. Two years ago he presented his budget to the county commissioners and outlined specific program goals. Last year, at another presentation, the commissioners asked about these goals in terms of achievement. Witherspoon had the information. So impressed were the commissioners, the mental health program was given every cent requested for it, an unprecedented occurrence in the area.

PROJECT SAGE—DENVER, COLORADO

Project Sage (Systems Approach to Goal Evaluation) is another illustration of key factor analysis in action. Eighty staff members at Denver's Fort Logan Mental Health Center have been trained in key factor analysis. In conceptual approach, development, and implementation it is similar to the North Carolina program. A new management by objectives system makes managers individually accountable for results—as they are in any modern corporation that manages to remain in the black. Capabilities have been generated by KFA that previously were unachievable.

The outline of specific goals, for example, and the development of measurement techniques now provide the methodology and data base with which to build an unprecedented degree of consumer satisfaction into center services. The consumer—patient, relative, friend—is asked at the outset what he hopes will be accomplished during treatment. The consumer sets his own goals at the beginning of treatment and again at one month. At discharge or 120 days after the beginning of treatment he is asked to evaluate how close the patient has come to accomplishing these goals by rating each one on the following one-to-six scale of attainment: (1) much further from, (2) further from, (3) no change, (4) somewhat closer, (5) much closer, (6) sufficient attainment. Of course, staff attainment goals are also used to plan individual treatment and to measure results.

As one recent study demonstrates, cost benefit techniques have made it possible to plot economic evaluation of such programs as treatment of alcoholics. Other accomplishments also have been impressive.

Dr. Ethel M. Bonn, director of the Fort Logan Mental Health Center, which serves the approximately one million residents of the Denver metropolitan area, is understandably enthusiastic—though professionally restrained in discussing the system. "I believe," she states, "that the principles of planning and measurement of goal attainment as used in Sage and similar approaches can be applied with benefit to the patient or client in any human services institution's work, such as health and mental health facilities, educational institutions, welfare, and other social service agencies. Training staff in utilizing the concepts and enlisting their commitment to making use of such approaches in planning is a crucial part of making such a system work successfully. From our experience, we know that taking the time and making the necessary efforts to achieve this kind of commitment are essential, and we feel, definitely worth it."

A SAMPLING OF ACTION SPECIFICS

What follows is a thought-starter rundown of action recommendations designed to accelerate the application of SEM principles to social institutions. To whom are these proposals addressed? To every citizen concerned about the future of our nation. Is there any one of us who has less of a stake in the survival of our democratic system than any other of us? The strategies for survival, to succeed, will require the dedicated and coordinated efforts of all America: government officials, businessmen, institutional directors and program administrators, social workers, professionals, rank and file people from office, warehouse, and plant. What follows is not an attempt at anything even faintly resembling a complete program of action. It is merely a collection of thoughts for consideration.

Action recommendation 1: Create exciting incentives
Whatever happened to the "good old-fashioned American ingenuity" that helped make America the most successful and prosperous free society on earth? In the old days, some say, innovators had more to gain from their ideas than they do today. Some strong arguments could be presented in support of this view. Be that as it may, the point is that it has been demonstrated on innumerable occasions that individuals, groups, institutions—anyone and everyone—can be inspired to greater productivity when the right plums are dangled. I think we need to devote considerably more time and effort to the task of dreaming up imaginative new incentives to inspire innovation and excellence. We need more industry experts, more "think tank" experts, more experts of all kinds studying and exploring new incentive techniques as well as new strategies for adapting and applying proven corporate incentives to the social sector.

Action recommendation 2: Cash in on over-60 expertise
There is a clear trend toward earlier executive retirement. IBM Chairman T. Vincent Learson retired at 60 and announced that henceforth all IBM corporate officers would bow out at that age. Dow Chemical reduced the retirement age of its 11 top officers to 60. Westinghouse did the same for its 7 top men. SKF's Chairman Thomas M. Rauch called it quits at age 50. Gulf's E. D. Brockett retired at 58. The trend presents an ex-

citing potential for social institutions. What more logical step —from private to public sector on a consulting capacity— could be imagined? The ideal transition for the dynamic executive who wants to slow down without spending the rest of his days on the golf course—and a boon for society. Just think of the talent and experience involved! It includes managers knowledgeable in the design of measurement techniques, technology transfer, incentive plan structuring, and merger and pruning strategies. It also includes planners, goal setters, and management scientists of every kind. What we need is an organized and coordinated national campaign to tap this priceless bank of over-60 talent and energy. The objective would be to match available manpower capabilities to institutional needs and establish the recruitment machinery to put these experts to work as planners, counselors, and guides for our social agencies.

Action recommendation 3: Refine and expand the art of technology transfer

Demonstrated similarities exist among social institutions in any given field. What pays off in one hospital, prison, or university will be adaptable to many other institutions across the country. But the first problem is to disseminate the information. This requires coordination and expertise at both the dispensing and receiving ends. As already mentioned, some states, cities, government agencies, and institutions are experimenting with aspects of technology transfer. A nonprofit, tax-exempt, Washington-based organization, Public Technology, Incorporated, was created in 1971 to serve as a research and development arm for state and local governments. PTI's goal is to apply the "world's most advanced science and technology to the solutions of city, country, and state problems." Innovations are disseminated nationwide via newsletter and other publications. It is an encouraging step. Multiplied by 100 or so, such efforts would go a long way toward improving our public institutions.

Action recommendation 4: Enlarge funding of social research groups

However simple and obvious the basic SEM principles, applying them to the public sector on a broad national basis will require considerable effort. It will be necessary to tailor the rules to specific institutions, dissolve natural resistance to change, sell restructuring to managers and administrators, and set up and operate modern management systems. Much experimentation will be needed, along with an analysis of better ways to define goals, measure progress, create incentives, train personnel, and educate the public. A number of groups have been formed in recent years with the function of social improvement in mind. These include the Organization for Social and Technical Innovation, Commission on the Year 2000, National Commission on the Causes and Prevention of Violence, Resources for the Future, Center for the Analysis of Public Issues, Harvard Program on Technology and Society, and many others. This is another encouraging sign of a blossoming awareness, but we need many more such organizations and programs. The key, of course, is enlarged funding—private, public, foundation—for new and existing groups, and for advanced methods in the assessment of programs to make certain the money is going where it will do the most good.

Action recommendation 5: Launch a "businessmen for SEM" movement

A key factor in the success of any movement or cause is the ability to stimulate public and political awareness regarding its value and importance. SEM is no exception. In the public sector especially, it is sometimes difficult to stir people out of their lethargy. It requires professional lobbying, effective marketing, and PR techniques to get the message across, to organize programs and attract the needed funding. "Businessmen for SEM" groups, strategically located from coast to coast, could do much toward expediting the development and implementation of SEM principles in local communities, and on the city, state, and federal levels.

Action recommendation 6: Educate young SEM activists

Today's business-oriented student gets at least a brief introduction in "Management I" to SEM principles. The young college person aspiring to a career in hospital management, social work, law enforcement, government, education, and other social fields receives little if any exposure to these management basics.

I think the academic community should act quickly to remedy this weakness. Social management courses should be created that not only introduce and explain sound management principles but, equally important, relate them to agency and institutional work and objectives.

Action recommendation 7: Sell Madison Avenue on "selling" America

The world's best products, from cuff links to condominiums, must be "sold" to the public if they are to gain acceptance. The advertising profession, through individual and association action, has repeatedly proved that its members are socially responsible citizens. Here's an outstanding opportunity for Madison Avenue to play a key role in triggering a turnaround in our unproductive social organizations. Why not a nationwide citizen education campaign designed to get the SEM story across to concerned individuals in all 50 states—triggered perhaps by the American Association of Advertising Agencies—via the networks and press? It would serve society mightily, and at the same time give the profession another important social commitment.

Action recommendation 8: Create "Distinguished Social Service" awards

I have mentioned a number of social agencies and institutions that, through the dedicated efforts of hard-working and selfless people, have produced remarkable improvement and restructuring. Certainly the men and women involved in such efforts deserve special recognition for outstanding achievement, and they should be given an incentive to do more of the same. I believe that such government funding agencies as OEO and HEW, along with the Office of the President, the networks, private foundations, such prestigious publications as *The New York Times, Harvard Business Review, Newsweek,* and *Time,* should create annual "Distinguished Social Service" awards for outstanding programs and efforts. The Distinguished Service Medal is conferred by the military for unusual heroism and sacrifice in war. Outstanding performance in America's socio-economic war for survival merits special attention as well.

Action recommendation 9: Expand SEM
task force activity

An abundance of evidence in this book and elsewhere demonstrates the improvement attainable when knowledgeable teams of professionals armed with the modern tools of management attack social problems. One need look no further for proof than to the job that was done in New York City's courts and schools by the task forces of business executives. When a strategy or approach succeeds, what could make more sense than to repeat it again and again? There is little question that the experiences in New York City, multiplied many times, would save billions of dollars and eliminate untold misery in the United States. It takes organization and funding to expand and coordinate such task force efforts, and to multiply progress through technology transfer. Can our nation afford not to make this investment?

Action recommendation 10: Activate
political support for SEM

The politician is admittedly dedicated to serving his constituency. But it is the nature of the political man to respond to the voices within his district that are loudest and most insistent. We already see many elected officials reacting with vigor and concern to public demands for better crime control, improved health care, a cleaner environment. But, as with the public at large, most politicians are uncertain as to what strategies would most effectively accomplish the desired results. Professional groups, businessmen's clubs, industry associations, and community groups, once they are enlightened as to the applicability of SEM to the social sector, could perform a vital service by taking up the crusade on a formal basis. We desperately need to get the message across to this nation's elected leaders on every level of government that what American institutions need now for a turnaround is Socio-Economic Management.

NOTES

CHAPTER 1

[Page 4]   Dr. Ritter's comments appeared in *The Morgan Guaranty Survey,* July 1971.

[Page 6]   The problems discussed by Charles L. Schultze and The Brookings Institution economists were published in "Setting National Priorities: The 1972 Budget," The Brookings Institution, Washington, D.C., May 1972.

[Page 8]   Margaret Mead was interviewed by Edwin Newman on WNBC's program "Speaking Freely," April 18, 1971.

CHAPTER 2

[Page 19]   Dr. Leon Lessenger's views were published in an article by June O'Neill, "Resources Use in Higher Education," Carnegie Commission on Higher Education, Berkeley, Calif., July 1971.

[Page 22]   Olson's comments are quoted from his address "The Relationship of Economics to the Other Social Sciences: The Province of a Social Report" (Annual Meeting of the American Political Sciences Association, Chicago, Ill., September 8, 1967).

[Page 24]   The dialog between Mr. Califano and Senator Mondale is from hearings before a Special Subcommittee on Evaluation and Planning of Social Programs of the Committee on Labor and Public Welfare, U.S. Senate, 91st Congress, Washington, D.C., December 18, 1969.

CHAPTER 3

[Page 39]   Rowen voiced his opinions to the author and before a Special Subcommittee on Evaluation and Planning of Social Pro-

grams of the Committee on Labor and Public Welfare, U.S. Senate, 91st Congress, Washington, D.C., December 18, 1969.
[Page 40]   Califano's views appeared in an article by Nathaniel Wollman, "The New Economics of Resources," *Daedalus*, Fall 1967, p. 1009.

CHAPTER 4

[Page 56]   Molinaro is quoted from his article "Truths and Consequences for Older Cities," *Saturday Review*, May 15, 1971, p. 30.
[Page 63]   Landsberg made these points in his article "Quantity and Quality in Resources," *Daedalus*, Fall 1967, p. 1055.

CHAPTER 5

[Page 68]   This experience was related in an article by George Cabot Lodge, "Top Priority: Renovating Our Ideology," *Harvard Business Review*, September–October 1970, p. 43.
[Page 69]   The views of Senator Mondale and other senators were reported in *The New York Times*, April 18, 1971.
[Page 70]   Tom Alexander's article appeared in *Fortune*, July 1969.
[Page 71]   *Future Shock*, Random House, New York, 1970, p. 1.
[Page 72]   Bower was quoted in "Improving Executive Management in the Federal Government," the Committee for Economic Development, New York, July 1964, p. 74.
[Page 75]   The Conference Board research report, "The Federal Budget—Its Impact on the Economy," was published in New York, 1968.

CHAPTER 6

[Page 83]   This discussion in *Future Shock* appears on pages 129–131.
[Page 84]   Cameron was quoted from *Fortune*, October 1971.
[Page 86]   Poston's statement is from his book *The Gang and the Establishment,* Harper & Row, New York, 1971, p. 232.
[Page 86]   Hayes made his statement at hearings before the Special Subcommittee on Evaluation and Planning of Social Programs, Washington, D.C., July 1969.

[Page 97]   Brewster's comments are from "The President's Annual Report," Yale University, Year-end 1970.

CHAPTER 7

[Page 101]   Anthony made his remarks in an address, "Can Non-
profit Organizations Be Well Managed?" (Boston University,
February 18, 1971).
[Page 103]   The situation prevailing in the communities constitut-
ing Valley View District 96 was reported in *The PTA Magazine*,
Chicago, Ill, March 1972.
[Page 107]   HUD's program was described in *Business Week*,
May 27, 1972.

CHAPTER 8

[Page 120]   Drucker's statement is from his book *The Age of
Discontinuity*, Harper & Row, New York, 1969, p. 196.
[Page 125]   Landsberg is quoted from his article "The U.S. Re-
source Outlook: Quantity," *Daedalus*, Fall 1967, p. 1046.
[Page 126]   The evaluation of outdoor recreation was reported in
a study by Ruth P. Mack and Sumner Myers, "Outdoor Recre-
ation," in *Measuring Benefits of Government Investments*, The
Brookings Institution, Washington, D.C., 1965.
[Page 128]   Quick's guidelines were described in *Fortune*, Febru-
ary 1972.

CHAPTER 9

[Page 143]   Ms. Carruth's attack on Governor Rockefeller's Al-
bany Mall program was reported in *Fortune*, June 1971.
[Page 144]   The material on teacher–student ratios is based on
an address by Alvin C. Eurich, "Education in the Seventies" (84th
Annual Meeting of the AICPA, Detroit, Mich., October 11, 1971).
[Page 147]   The Van Der Hueven clinic was described in *Atlas*,
November 1971, p. 28.

CHAPTER 10

[Page 156]   Wollman's statement is from his article "The New
Economics of Resources," *Daedalus*, Fall 1967, p. 1009.

[Page 157] Champion stated his views in an address, "New Dimensions in Urban Action" (New York Chamber of Commerce, June 3, 1971).

[Page 157] A report on the Economic Development Council's task force was published in James Nathan Miller's article "Reprieve for New York's Criminal Courts," *National Civic Review*, March 1972.

[Page 158] Franklin Lindsay is quoted from his article "Management and the Total Environment," *Columbia Journal of World Business*, January–February 1970.

[Page 160] The Brownstone Revival Committee's activities are described in "Urban Action" (semiannual report of the Economic Development Council of New York City, June–December 1971).

[Page 161] The comments by William Gorham were excerpted from his testimony at hearings of the Subcommittee on Government Research, Committee on Government Operations, Washington, D.C., July 26, 1967.

[Page 162] David Rockefeller made his statement in an address, "The Era of Growing Business Accountability" (Advertising Council, New York, December 13, 1971).

CHAPTER 12

[Page 184] The young writer who participated in Budd Schulberg's workshop is Johnie Scott, "My Home Is Watts," *Harper's*, October 1966, p. 47.

CHAPTER 13

[Page 204] The hospital study was discussed by Donald W. Spalding at an American Medical Association meeting, September 13, 1972.

[Page 206] The CASH project was described in *Modern Hospital*, October 1972.

[Page 207] The "Four Cities" program was the topic of an address by Dr. H. Guyford Stever (American Institute of Aeronautics and Astronautics, Washington, D.C., September 22, 1972).

[Page 208] The 1968 consolidation of eight Phoenix-area hospitals into the Samaritan Health Services system was reported in a fact sheet released by Health Services Research Center, Phoenix, Ariz., July 27, 1972.

[Page 210] The results of TEMP are discussed in "Annual Report: Tennessee Effective Management Program, 1971–1972."

INDEX